MATH SERIES

by Vicky Rene Kirkpatrick

Dedicated to David, Marshall, and Thomas.

Published by
Garlic Press
100 Hillview Lane #2
Eugene, OR 97401

ISBN 0-931993-54-7
Order Number GP-054

Contents

Congruent figures are figures that are the same in size and shape. Figures are congruent when each line segment and each angle are in the same relative position. Parts of figures that are in the same relative position are called **corresponding parts**.

The symbol, or notation, for congruency is ≅. Finding congruent figures can help to identify unknown measurements.

Any figure or shape can have a matching congruent partner.

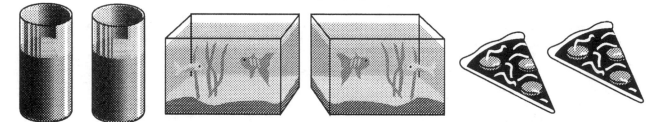

Figure I is congruent to Figure II.

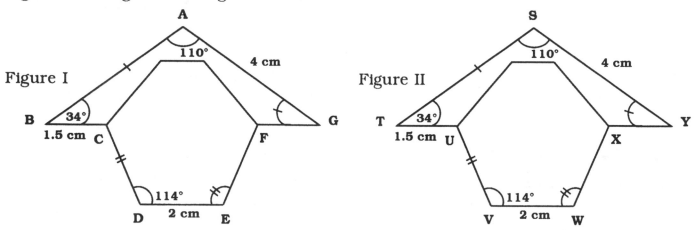

Here is a list of some corresponding parts (angles and sides) from Figure I and Figure II and their measurements.

•Corresponding Angles

∠A	= ∠S	= 110°
∠B	= ∠T	= 34°
∠D	= ∠V	= 114°
∠G	= ∠Y	Notice how these angles have been marked with one dash. The dash indicates that the angles are equal even though we do not know their measurements.
∠E	= ∠W	Both are marked with two dashes.

• Corresponding Sides

$\overline{AG} = \overline{SY} = 4$ cm
$\overline{BC} = \overline{TU} = 1.5$ cm
$\overline{DE} = \overline{VW} = 2$ cm
$\overline{AB} = \overline{ST} =$ both are marked with one dash.
$\overline{CD} = \overline{UV} =$ both are marked with two dashes.

We know that Figure I is congruent to Figure II. And we know that all corresponding parts are equal. From these two facts, we can conclude:
$\angle C = \angle U$ and $\overline{EF} = \overline{WX}$ even though they are not marked with dashes or with measurements.

Figures need not be in the same position to be congruent. Notice how the second figure below has been rotated. Despite the rotation, the figures are still congruent to each other.

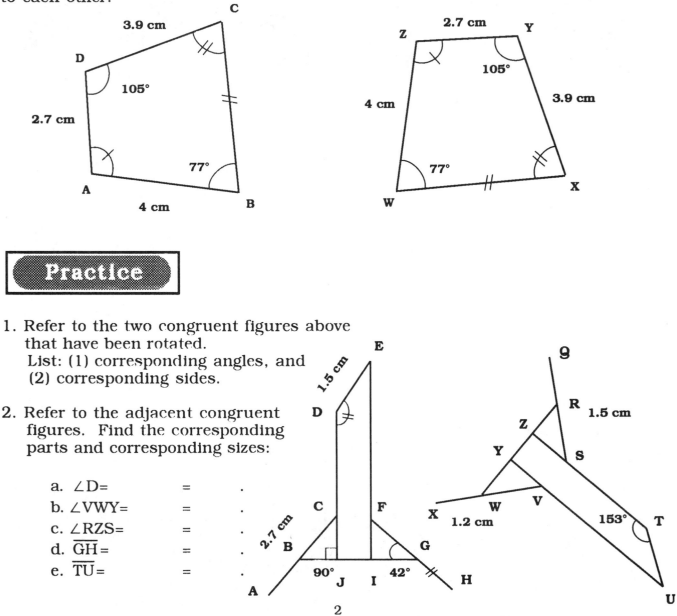

Practice

1. Refer to the two congruent figures above that have been rotated.
   List: (1) corresponding angles, and (2) corresponding sides.

2. Refer to the adjacent congruent figures. Find the corresponding parts and corresponding sizes:

   a. $\angle D =$ _____ = _____ .
   b. $\angle VWY =$ _____ = _____ .
   c. $\angle RZS =$ _____ = _____ .
   d. $\overline{GH} =$ _____ = _____ .
   e. $\overline{TU} =$ _____ = _____ .

2

Congruent Triangles

Congruent triangles occur often and they can be used to find missing information.

Let's take a detailed look at two congruent triangles and then discuss short cuts to show congruency.

The first triangle, ΔABC, is congruent to the second triangle, ΔDEF, because all corresponding parts are equal.

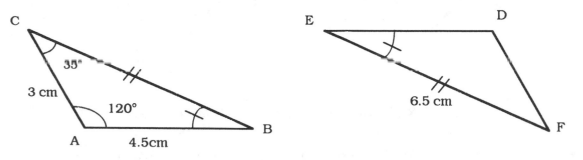

$\overline{AB}$ corresponds to $\overline{DE}$. They are in the same relative position on the congruent triangles. We can conclude that $\overline{AB} = \overline{DE} = 4.5$ cm.

Since $\overline{BC}$ corresponds to $\overline{EF}$ then : $\overline{BC} = \overline{EF} = 6.5$ cm.

$\overline{CA}$ corresponds to $\overline{FD}$, so : $\overline{CA} = \overline{FD} = 3$ cm.

Each triangle, by definition, has three angles. Angle A can be written ∠ A, or as ∠CAB, or as ∠ BAC. Angle A is formed by $\overline{CA}$ and $\overline{AB}$. These sides correspond to $\overline{FD}$ and $\overline{DE}$ which form ∠D. Since ∠A and ∠D are in the same relative position on the congruent triangles, they are corresponding and equal: ∠A = ∠D = 120°.

Angle C can be written as ∠C, or as ∠ACB, or as ∠BCA. It corresponds to ∠F. Angle C = ∠F = 35°.

Angle B can be written as ∠B, or as ∠ABC, or as ∠CBA. It corresponds to ∠E. Angle B = ∠E = ? This measurement is not given, but we can still find its size.

The sum of all three angles in any triangle is 180°. Given angles that measure 120° and 35°, the third angle is 25°, since: 180° - 120° - 35° = 25°.

In summary: So far, to determine if figures are congruent, we have compared all corresponding sides and angles to see if they are equal. However, with triangles, we need not compare all the parts. There are shortcuts to check congruency of triangles.

◀ Side-Side-Side (SSS) Property

If triangles have three corresponding sides that are equal, then the triangles are congruent. We can also conclude that the corresponding angles are equal without having to measure them. This condition is call the **side-side-side property of congruent triangles**, or the **SSS Property**.

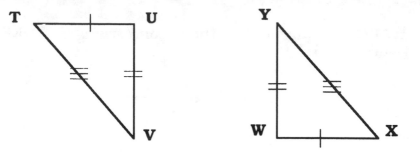

ΔTUV $\cong$ ΔXWY by SSS (side-side-side) Property.

Given that the three sides are congruent, we can conclude that the three angles are also congruent without measuring them:

$$\angle T \quad = \quad \angle X$$
$$\angle U \quad = \quad \angle W$$
$$\angle V \quad = \quad \angle Y$$

1. Why are the following two triangles congruent? List all corresponding sides and angles.

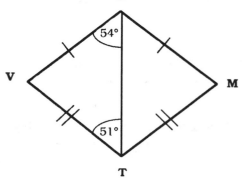

4

◀Side-Angle-Side (SAS) Property

If two triangles have two corresponding sides equal and the corresponding angle between the sides is equal, then the triangles are congruent. We can conclude also that the other corresponding parts are equal without measuring them. This condition is called the **side-angle-side property of congruent triangles** or the **SAS Property**.

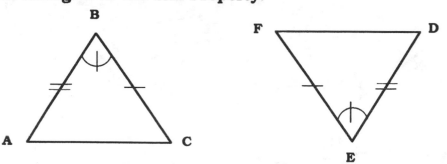

Given that $\overline{AB} = \overline{DE}$ and $\overline{BC} = \overline{EF}$ as equal corresponding sides and $\angle B = \angle E$ as equal corresponding angles BETWEEN the given equal sides,
then $\triangle ABC \cong \triangle DEF$ by SAS.

We can conclude: $\overline{AC} = \overline{DF}$ $\angle A = \angle D$ $\angle C = \angle F$
as corresponding parts of congruent triangles.

1. Are these triangles congruent? Why or Why not?

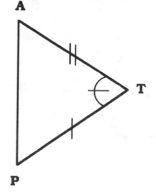

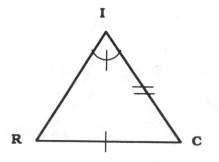

◀Angle-Side Angle (ASA) Property

If triangles have two equal corresponding angles and an equal corresponding side, then the triangles are congruent. We can conclude that the other corresponding parts are equal without measuring them. This condition is called the **angle-side-angle property of congruent triangles**, or the **ASA Property**.

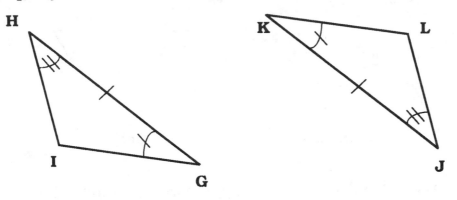

Given that $\angle G = \angle K$ and $\angle H = \angle J$ are equal corresponding angles and $\overline{GH} = \overline{JK}$ are equal corresponding sides, then $\triangle GIH \cong \triangle KLJ$ by ASA.

We can conclude: $\angle I = \angle L$ $\overline{GI} = \overline{KL}$ $\overline{IH} = \overline{LJ}$
as corresponding parts of congruent triangles.

The equal corresponding side does not have to be between two equal corresponding angles. The following triangles are congruent even though the corresponding equal sides are not between the two given angles.

Consider these two congruent triangles.

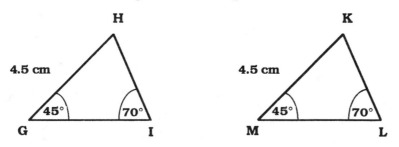

This could be noted as a SAA or AAS condition.

Given that $\angle G = \angle M = 45°$ and $\angle I = \angle L = 70°$, then both $\angle H$ and $\angle K$ must equal 65°, since $180° - 45° - 70° = 65°$.

6

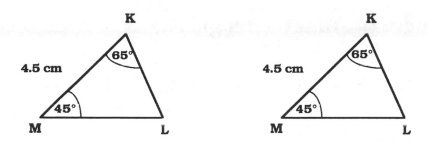

But, in this situation, the SAA or AAS notation becomes the ASA Property.

Practice

1. If the triangles below are congruent, find the size of all the parts of both triangles.

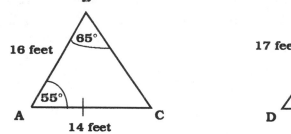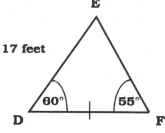

2. Is △ABE ≅ △DBC? Why or why not?

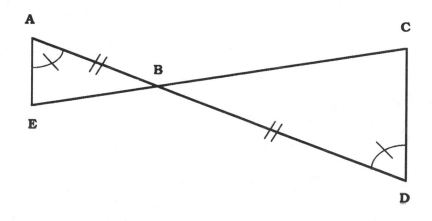

Congruent Right Triangles

The SSS, ASA, and SAS properties also apply to right triangles, although the properties may be written with different letters. There is also a congruency property that is unique to right triangles.

First, let's identify the parts of a right triangle. One of the angles measures 90° and is usually marked with a box at the angle:

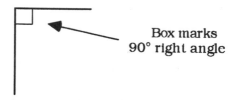

Box marks
90° right angle

The side opposite the 90° angle is called the **hypotenuse**. The hypotenuse is always the longest side. The other two sides are usually called **legs**.

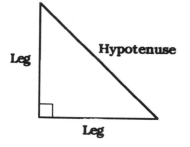

Using the vocabulary of right triangles, notice how the letters of the congruent properties can be changed:

◀**LL Property**

Consider these congruent triangles:

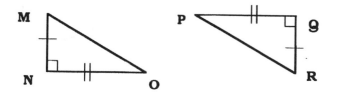

$\overline{MN}$ = $\overline{RQ}$ as they are equal corresponding sides.
∠N = ∠Q as they are both right angles.
$\overline{NO}$ = $\overline{QP}$ as they are equal corresponding sides.

So, ΔMNO ≅ ΔRQP by SAS.

8

Since the sides of a right triangle are called legs, we could write SAS (side-angle-side) as LAL (leg-angle-leg). And since that included angle is a right angle in both triangles, all we need to write is LL (leg-leg).

Consider these congruent right triangles.

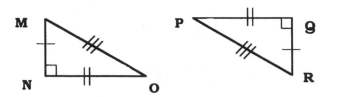

$\triangle MNO \cong \triangle RQP$ by SSS. But since both are right triangles, we know they both have a right angle. SSS becomes SASS which can become SAS or LL.

So, for right triangles, the SAS property and the SSS property can be called the LL property.

◀ LA Property

Consider these two congruent right triangles.

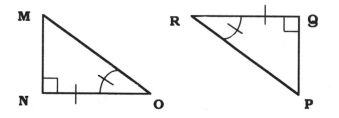

$\angle N = \angle Q$ as right angles.
$\overline{NO} = \overline{RQ}$ as equal corresponding sides.
$\angle O = \angle R$ as equal corresponding angles.

$\triangle MNO \cong \triangle PQR$ by ASA.

We could express ASA (angle-side-angle) as ALA (angle-leg-angle). And since we know they both have right angles, we can shorten this to LA (leg-angle).

◀ HA Property

Consider these two congruent right triangles.

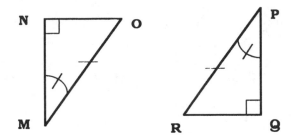

∠M = ∠P as given corresponding angles.

$\overline{MO}$ = $\overline{PR}$ as given corresponding hypotenuse.

∠N = ∠Q as right angles.

∠O = ∠R Remember, given two angles as congruent, we know that the third angles are also congruent.

ΔMNO ≅ ΔPQR by ASA. The ASA could be written as AHA (angle-hypotenuse-angle). This can be shortened to HA (hypotenuse-angle). (Only right triangles have an hypotenuse).

◀ HL Property

The next property is unique to right triangles.

(Note: this property does not imply that there is a related ASS or SSA property for other triangles. See the Ambiguous Cases section in section 3 of this chapter.)

Consider these two right triangles. Given equal hypotenuse and one pair of equal legs, are these triangles congruent?

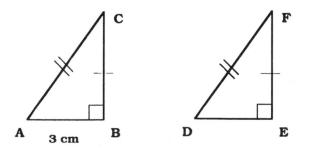

If we can show that ΔABC and ΔDEF are both congruent to a third triangle, then we can conclude they are congruent to each other.

We are now considering three right triangles. Starting with ΔDEF, we'll form a third triangle by drawing line FG and line EG. Thus, $\overline{EG} = \overline{AB}$ = 3 cm and ∠G = ∠D. Notice that ΔFEG is also a right triangle.

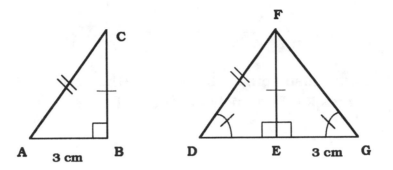

Notice that : $\overline{AB} = \overline{EG}$ = 3cm.

∠ABC = ∠GEF = 90°.

$\overline{BC} = \overline{EF}$ as both are marked with one dash.

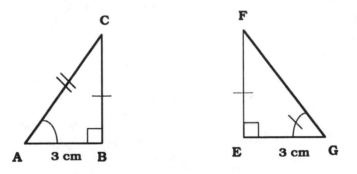

Because of these equal corresponding parts, we can conclude ΔABC ≅ ΔGEF by SAS or LL as they are right triangles. Now we know that $\overline{AC} = \overline{FG}$ as they are corresponding parts of congruent triangles.

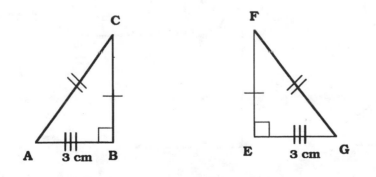

11

Consider triangles DEF and GEF.

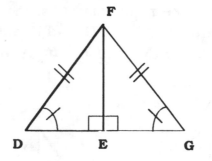

These triangles are also congruent because they are right triangles with one pair of equal corresponding angles and equal hypotenuse.

$\triangle DEF \cong \triangle GEF$ by HA.

Since both of the original triangles (ABC and DEF) are congruent to $\triangle GEF$, they are congruent to each other.

$\triangle ABC \cong \triangle DEF$ by HL.

Practice

1. Are these right triangles congruent? Why or why not?

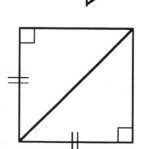

2. Are these right triangles congruent? Why or why not?

3. Are these right triangles congruent? Why or why not?

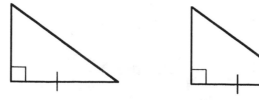

Be careful of a situation where two sides are congruent and one angle is congruent but that angle is not included between the congruent sides. This condition does not prove congruency for triangles that are not right triangles.

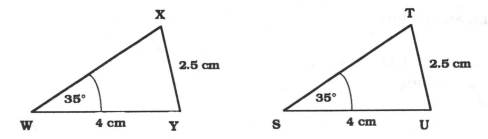

ΔWXY is not necessarily congruent to ΔSTU. These two triangles could look like this:

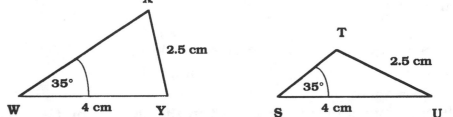

This condition of ASS or SSA is called ambiguous because it could apply to several triangles that may or may not be congruent. In this situation, further measurements must be made to ensure congruency.

Be aware of another situation: when all three angles of one triangle are equal to the three angles of another triangle. This conditon of AAA does not prove congruency, the sides of the triangle could be different.

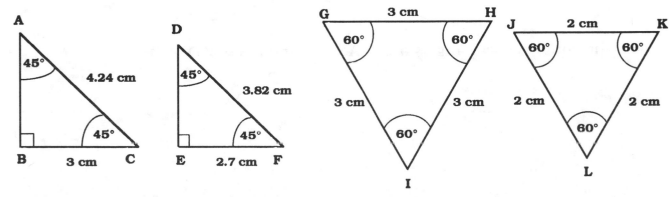

ΔABC is NOT congruent to ΔDEF. ΔGHI is NOT congruent with ΔJLK.

Figures are congruent if their corresponding sides are equal and their corresponding angles are equal.

The symbol ≅ means congruent.

Properties of congruent triangles are

ASA   angle-side-angle
SSS   side-side-side
SAS   side-angle-side.   Be sure the angle is included between the sides.

Congruent properties for right triangles are

HL   hypotenuse-leg
LL   leg-leg
HA   hypotenuse-angle   (Not the right angle.)
LA   leg-angle   (Not the right angle.)

The sum of all angles in any triangle is 180°. Given the size of any two angles of a triangle, the third angle can be found by subtracting the given two measures from 180°.

Vertical angles are formed by two intersecting lines, and they are equal in size.

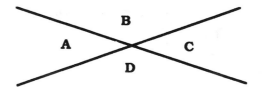

The equal vertical angles are: ∠A = ∠C and ∠B = ∠D.

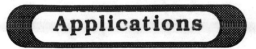

Let's put these congruency properties to use. Be careful though, sometimes pictures are not drawn accurately. They may be distorted. Don't rely on just looking at them. Refer to given measurements or notations to be sure of congruent, corresponding parts.

1. Is △DEC ≅ △FEC? Why?

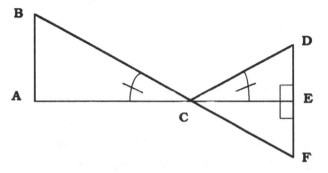

2. If a diagonal is drawn in this parallelogram, will the two triangles formed be congruent? Why or why not?

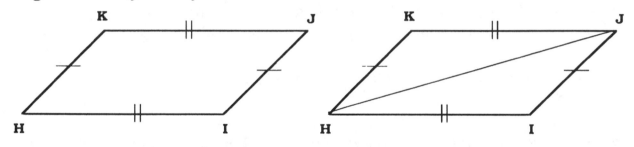

3. If a diagonal is drawn in this trapezoid, will the two triangles formed be congruent? Why or why not?

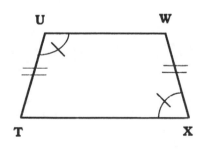
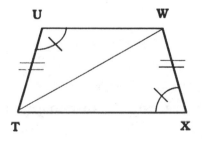

4. Is △AFE ≅ △BCD? Why or why not?

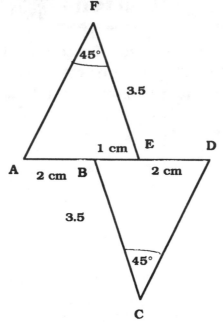

5. Matt rented a wind surfing board with a triangular sail. He wanted to know what the measurements of the three sides were, but he could only measure the bottom side and two bottom angles.

His friend, Dave, also had a windsurfing board and knew all the measurements. Can Dave help Matt find the size of the other two sides of Matt's sail?

Hint: Draw a picture of the two sails and label the parts that Juan can measure.

6. Amy needed to know the distance across a hole in the ground that was inaccessible to direct measurement.

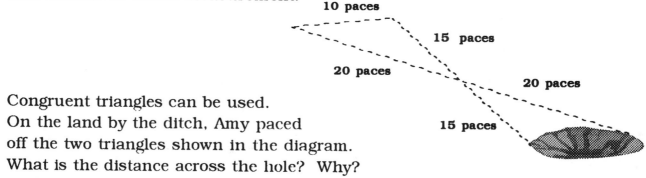

Congruent triangles can be used.
On the land by the ditch, Amy paced
off the two triangles shown in the diagram.
What is the distance across the hole? Why?

16

7. When erecting a center pole which is perpendicular to the ground and which is at the back end of a tent, what minimal measurements would you take to ensure that the pole is centered? What would you measure and why does that measurement show that the pole is centered?

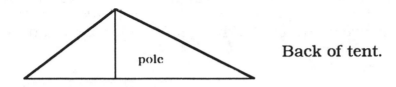 Back of tent.

Properties of Polygons

Polygons are formed by enclosing an area with straight sides. Polygons are used often and they have unique, identifying characteristics. As we discuss them, notice how the different parts relate to each other and how we can add auxiliary lines to enhance other relationships.

These are polygons.

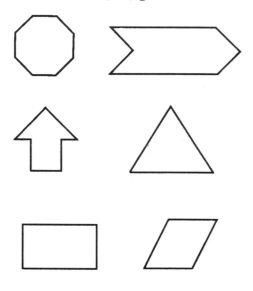

These are NOT polygons.

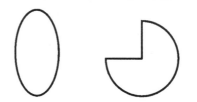

The sides are not straight.

The sides do not enclose an area.

Polygons are named according to how many sides they have.

Number of Sides	Name
3	triangle
4	quadrilateral
5	pentagon
6	hexagon
8	octagon
10	decagon
n	n-sided polygon or n-gon

A polygon with 18 sides could be called an 18-gon.

If a polygon has sides that are equal in measurement and all angle measurements are equal, the polygon is called **regular**.

Name these regular polygons:

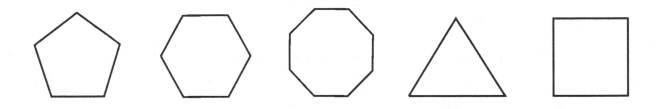

---

1 | **Triangles and Proofs**

We worked with triangles in Chapter 1. There are still more characteristics to learn about triangles.

Some characteristics will be explained using a simple proof. A **proof** consists of given facts and information that must be explained in detail, step-by-step, to justify a **statement**. This explanation can include definitions or previously established facts.

The statements to be proven can be put into an *if...then* form. For example: *If* a triangle is an isosceles triangle, *then* it has two equal base angles. The *if* part ("a triangle is an isosceles triangle") is the given fact; the *then* part ("two equal base angles") needs to be proven.

An isosceles triangle has two sides of equal length. This fact forces a condition on the angles, as we will show in a proof.

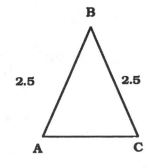

Proof: *If* AB = BC, *then* ∠A = C.   (The *if* part is the given fact and the *then* part is what we must prove.)

First, draw an auxiliary line from B to the middle of AC. This auxiliary line forms congruent triangles that can be used to provide missing information about pieces of the figure.

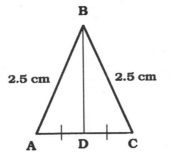

Next, list all of the facts or relationships about the figure and a reason for the relationship.

AB = BC   as the given equal sides of the isosceles triangle.
AD = DC   as drawn.
BD = BD   as it is the same line.

So, $\triangle ADB \cong \triangle CDB$ by SSS. We can therefore conclude that $\angle A = \angle C$. They are corresponding parts of congruent triangles.

Triangle Inequality

Triangle inequality states a fact about the lengths of the sides of any triangle. Two sides added together will always be greater than the length of the third side.

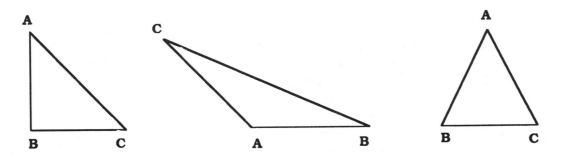

AB + BC > CA and BC + CA > AB and CA + AB > BC

For all triangles, when any two sides are added together, their sum will always be greater than the third side.

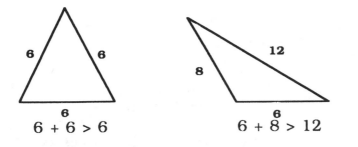

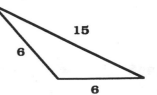

6 + 6 > 6   6 + 8 > 12   6 + 6 ⊁ 15. This drawing is distorted. There can't be a $\triangle$ with sides 6, 6, and 15.

20

Midpoints of Sides

There is another relationship between the sides of a triangle. To illustrate, first locate the point that bisects each side. This midpoint divides the side into two equal segments.

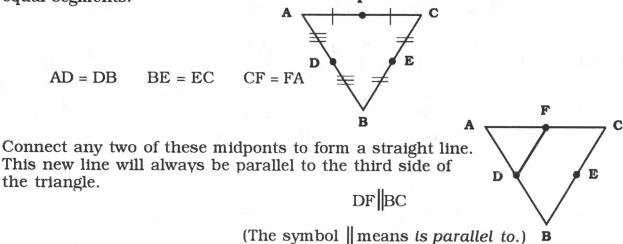

AD = DB   BE = EC   CF = FA

Connect any two of these midponts to form a straight line. This new line will always be parallel to the third side of the triangle.

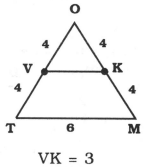

DF∥BC

(The symbol ∥ means *is parallel to*.)

This new line formed will also be half as long as the third side of the triangle.

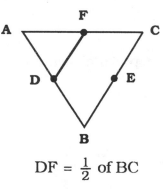

DF = $\frac{1}{2}$ of BC

VK = 3
VK ∥ TM

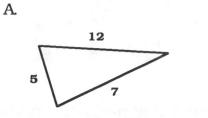

What is wrong with each picture?

A.

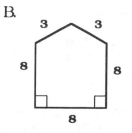

B.

C.

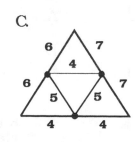

21

Polygons with four sides are **quadrilaterals**. Some quadrilaterals have special names and special characteristics that will be discussed in this chapter.

A **trapezoid** is a quadrilateral with one set of opposite sides that is parallel. These parallel sides are not equal in length.

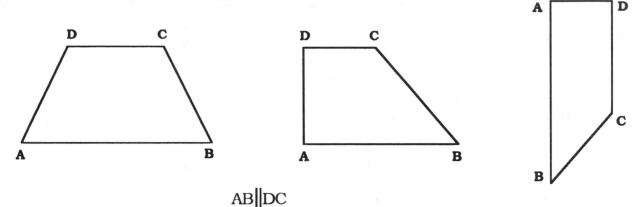

AB∥DC

Isosceles Trapezoid

In an isosceles trapezoid the two sides that are not parallel are equal in length. ∠A and ∠B are called base angles.

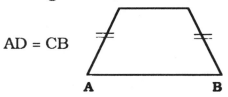

AD = CB

In an isosceles trapezoid the base angles are equal as shown in the following proof:

Fill in the missing details for this proof:

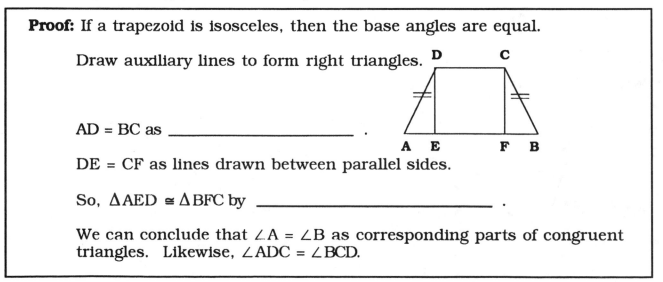

Proof: If a trapezoid is isosceles, then the base angles are equal.

Draw auxiliary lines to form right triangles.

AD = BC as _____ .

DE = CF as lines drawn between parallel sides.

So, △AED ≅ △BFC by _____ .

We can conclude that ∠A = ∠B as corresponding parts of congruent triangles. Likewise, ∠ADC = ∠BCD.

Midpoints of Sides

In a trapezoid, we can connect the midpoints of the two non-parallel sides to form a line. In any trapezoid this line is called the **median**. The median is parallel to the two parallel sides of the trapezoid.

The median is also equal to half the sum of the two parallel sides.

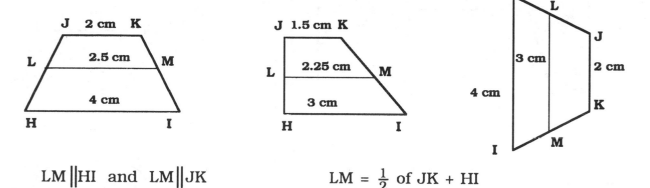

$$LM \parallel HI \ \text{and} \ LM \parallel JK \qquad\qquad LM = \tfrac{1}{2} \ \text{of} \ JK + HI$$

```
Property of Trapezoids

One set of opposite sides is parallel.
```

Given ABCD is a trapezoid, Find the length of EF.

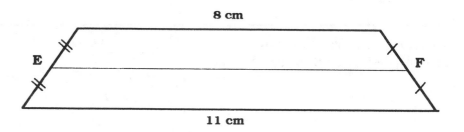

8 cm

E   F

11 cm

A **parallelogram** is a quadrilateral with opposite sides equal and parallel.

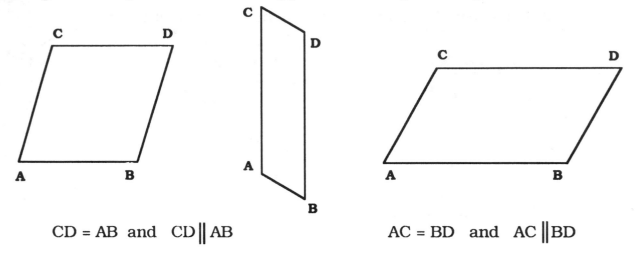

$$CD = AB \quad \text{and} \quad CD \parallel AB \qquad\qquad AC = BD \quad \text{and} \quad AC \parallel BD$$

Angles of a Parallelogram

We can add a line to our parallelogram to illustrate unique characteristics. A line from one angle of a polygon to another is called a **diagonal**.

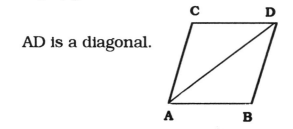

AD is a diagonal.

If a quadrilateral is a parallelogram, then what can we say about opposite angles? The following proof will explain opposite angles:

Proof: If ABCD is a parallelogram, then opposite angles are equal.

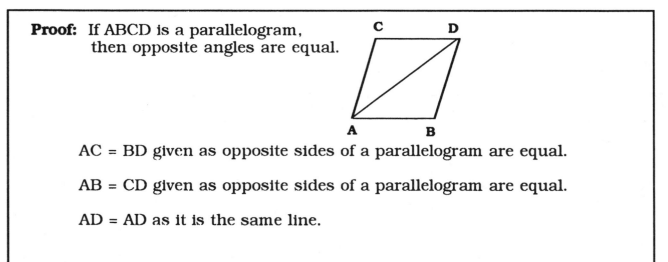

AC = BD given as opposite sides of a parallelogram are equal.

AB = CD given as opposite sides of a parallelogram are equal.

AD = AD as it is the same line.

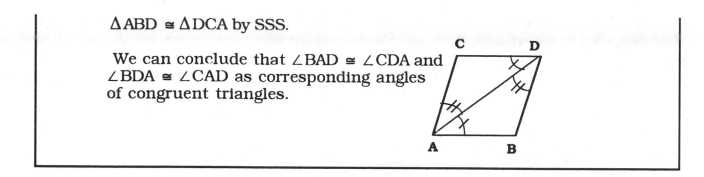

$\triangle$ABD $\cong$ $\triangle$DCA by SSS.

We can conclude that $\angle$BAD $\cong$ $\angle$CDA and $\angle$BDA $\cong$ $\angle$CAD as corresponding angles of congruent triangles.

These angles are also called equal **alternate interior angles** as they are formed by a diagonal (or **transversal**) drawn between two parallel lines.

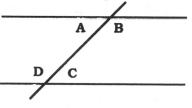

$\angle$A = $\angle$C and $\angle$D = $\angle$B as alternate interior angles between parallel lines.

Diagonals of a Parallelogram

If we draw both diagonals, we can show that they bisect each other (divide each other in half). Witness the following proof. Fill in missing details, too.

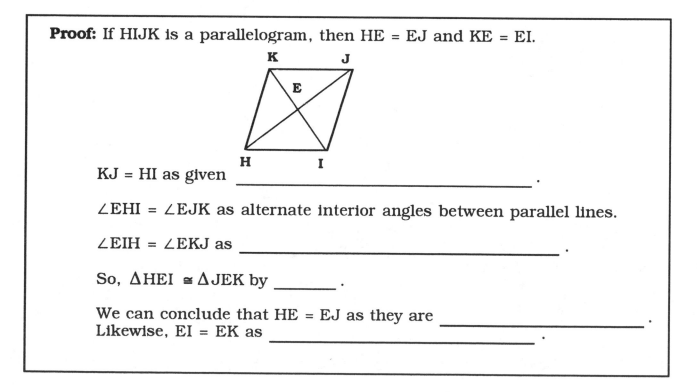

Proof: If HIJK is a parallelogram, then HE = EJ and KE = EI.

KE = HI as given _____.

$\angle$EHI = $\angle$EJK as alternate interior angles between parallel lines.

$\angle$EIH = $\angle$EKJ as _____.

So, $\triangle$HEI $\cong$ $\triangle$JEK by _____.

We can conclude that HE = EJ as they are _____.
Likewise, EI = EK as _____.

While we can conclude that diagonals bisect each other, we can not conclude that the diagonals are both equal. Even though STUV is a parallelogram, VT is not equal to SU.

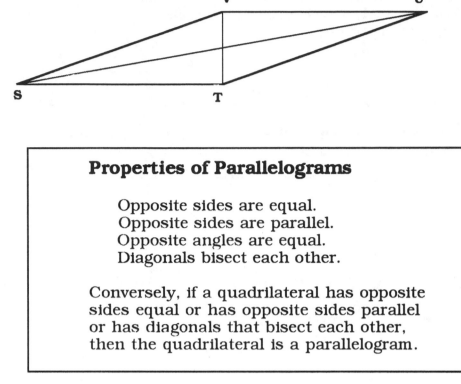

Properties of Parallelograms

Opposite sides are equal.
Opposite sides are parallel.
Opposite angles are equal.
Diagonals bisect each other.

Conversely, if a quadrilateral has opposite sides equal or has opposite sides parallel or has diagonals that bisect each other, then the quadrilateral is a parallelogram.

Practice

1. Given that ABCD is a parallelogram and given that the sum of all the angles of a quadrilateral equals 360°, find the measurment of ∠B, ∠C, and ∠D.

2. Given that ABCD is a parallelogram, prove that △DEC ≅ △AEB.

A rectangle is also a quadrilateral that has opposite sides equal and parallel. Thus, we can classify a rectangle as a parallelogram. What makes a rectangle unique is the fact that it has 90° angles.

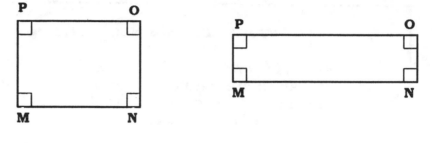

$$PO = MN \quad \text{and} \quad PO \parallel MN$$
$$PM = NO \quad \text{and} \quad PM \parallel NO$$
$$\angle M = \angle N = \angle O = \angle P = 90°$$

Diagonals of a Rectangle

Another unique characteristic of a rectangle involves diagonals. Follow this proof. Fill in the blanks.

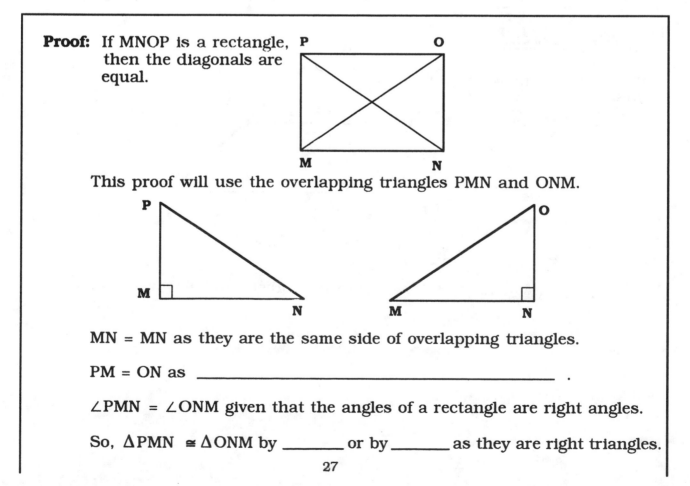

Proof: If MNOP is a rectangle, then the diagonals are equal.

This proof will use the overlapping triangles PMN and ONM.

MN = MN as they are the same side of overlapping triangles.

PM = ON as _____ .

∠PMN = ∠ONM given that the angles of a rectangle are right angles.

So, △PMN ≅ △ONM by _____ or by _____ as they are right triangles.

We can conclude that PN = OM as corresponding parts of congruent triangles.

For any rectangle, the diagonals are equal to each other.

Properties of a Rectangle

Opposite sides are equal.
Opposite sides are parallel.   These are the qualities of a
Opposite angles are equal.   parallelogram.
Diagonals bisect each other.

All angles are 90°.   These qualities are
Diagonals are equal.   unique to rectangles.

Conversely, if a parallelogram has equal diagonals or has 90° angles, then it is a rectangle.

1. What kind of quadrilateral is BFDC? Why?

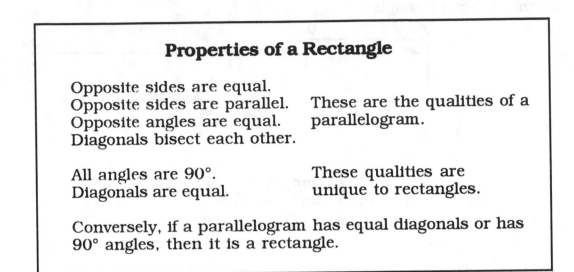

2. What properties does a rectangle have that other parallelograms do not have?

A **rhombus** is a quadrilateral with opposite sides equal and parallel. A rhombus is also a parallelogram. What makes a rhombus unique from other parallelograms is that all four of its sides are equal.

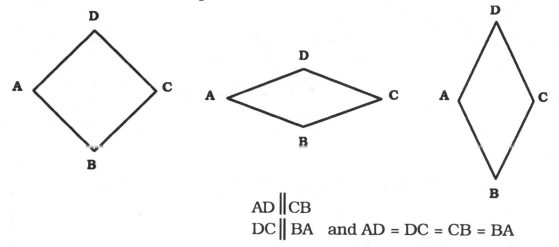

$$AD \parallel CB$$
$$DC \parallel BA \quad \text{and } AD = DC = CB = BA$$

Diagonals of a Rhombus

The diagonals of a rhombus have a unique property as shown in the following proof. The proof will first show that the diagonals form equal angles, that these angles form a straight angle, and conclude that the diagonals are perpendicular to each other.

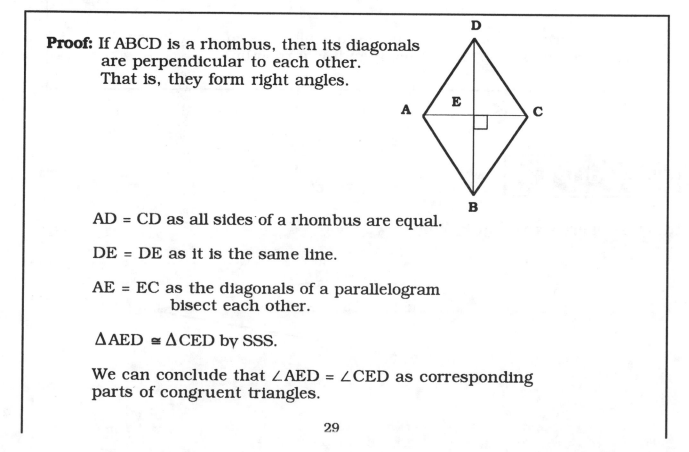

Proof: If ABCD is a rhombus, then its diagonals are perpendicular to each other. That is, they form right angles.

AD = CD as all sides of a rhombus are equal.

DE = DE as it is the same line.

AE = EC as the diagonals of a parallelogram bisect each other.

$\triangle AED \cong \triangle CED$ by SSS.

We can conclude that $\angle AED = \angle CED$ as corresponding parts of congruent triangles.

29

These two angles also form a straight line or a straight angle. The measurement of a straight angle is 180°.

If two angles are equal and add to 180°, then they are both 90°. This means that they are perpendicular to each other.

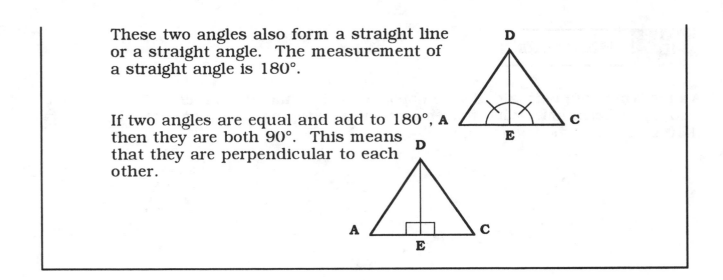

Properties of a Rhombus

Opposite sides are equal.
Opposite sides are parallel.
Opposite angles are equal.
Diagonals bisect each other.

These are the qualities of a parallelogram.

All sides are equal.
Diagonals are perpendicular to each other.

These qualities are unique to a rhombus.

Conversely, if a parallelogram has all sides equal or it has perpendicular diagonals, then it is a rhombus.

1. Is this figure a rhombus? Why or why not?

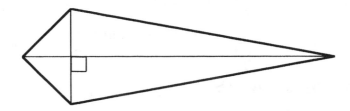

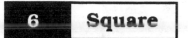

6   **Square**

Squares are quadrilaterals that have opposite sides equal and parallel. Thus, squares can be classified as parallelograms. Squares have 90° angles, so squares are also rectangles. The diagonals of a square are perdendicular, so a square can also be classified as a rhombus. As a rhombus, all four sides of a square are equal as shown in the following proof.

Fill in the details of the following proof.

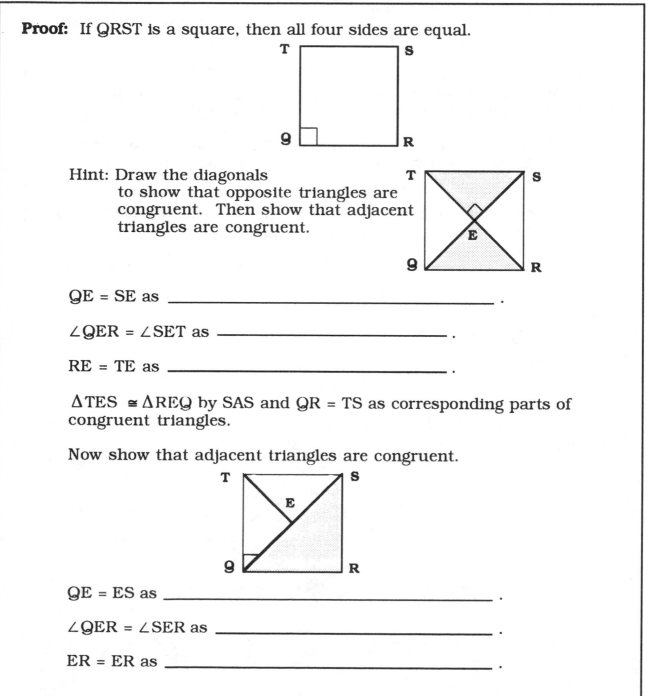

Proof: If QRST is a square, then all four sides are equal.

Hint: Draw the diagonals to show that opposite triangles are congruent. Then show that adjacent triangles are congruent.

QE = SE as _____ .

∠QER = ∠SET as _____ .

RE = TE as _____ .

ΔTES ≅ ΔREQ by SAS and QR = TS as corresponding parts of congruent triangles.

Now show that adjacent triangles are congruent.

QE = ES as _____ .

∠QER = ∠SER as _____ .

ER = ER as _____ .

31

$\triangle QER \cong \triangle SER$ by _____ or by _____ . QR = SR as corresponding parts of congruent triangles.

Since QR = SR and QR = TS, then SR = TS and we can see that SR = TS = QR = TQ.

Properties of a Square

Opposite sides are equal.
Opposite sides are parallel.
Opposite angles are equal.
Diagonals bisect each other.

These are the qualities of a parallelogram.

All angles are 90°
Diagonals are equal.

These are the qualities of a rectangle.

All sides are equal.
Diagonals are perpendicular to each other.

These qualities are unique to a rhombus.

Conversely, if a parallelogram has the characteristics of both a rectangle and a rhombus, then it is a square.

Practice

1. What is the most specific name for this figure? And what are the measurements of sides AB, BC, and DC? (Note: the drawing is distorted.)

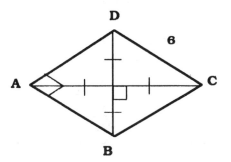

Angles within polygons have interesting relationships. We already know that the angles in any triangle add up to 180°. We can use this fact to find the sum of angles in any polygon.

In any polygon we can draw diagonals from one vertex, or angle, to all other vertices. Notice that a diagonal cannot be drawn to adjacent vertices.

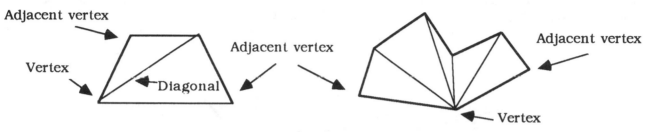

When diagonals are drawn, triangles are formed. We can add the sum of angles in each triangle to find the sum of all the angles in the polygon.

In any quadrilateral two triangles are formed, and the sum of all the angles in that quadrilateral is: 2 x 180° = 360°.

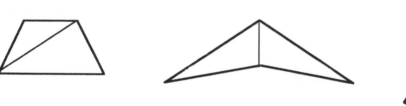
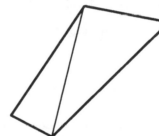

In any pentagon, three triangles are formed and the sum of all angles is: 3 x 180° = 540°.

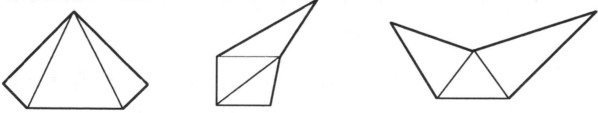

In any octagon, six triangles are formed and the sum of all the angles is: 6 x 180° = 1080°.

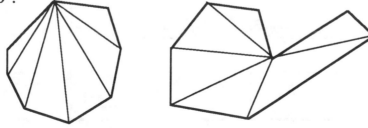

Instead of drawing the diagonals, we can use a formula to determine the sum of all angles in any polygon.

A polygon has the same number of angles as it has sides. If a polygon has N sides, it also has N angles (N stands for an unknown amount).

When the triangles are formed there are always two less than the number of angles contained in the polygon. This is because the diagonal is not connected to the two adjacent angles. If a polygon has N sides, the diagonal will connect N-2 angles and form N-2 triangles. The formula is: (N-2)180° = sum of all angles.

An example: If a polygon has 12 sides, then there are 12 - 2 = 10 triangles formed. The sum of all the angles is (12 - 2) x 180° = 1800°.

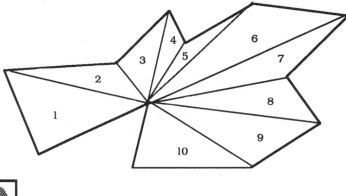

Practice

Fill in the chart using the formula: (N-2)180° = sum of all angles.

Number of polygon sides.	Number of angles.	Number of triangles formed.	Sum of all angles in the polygon.
4	4	2	2 x 180° = _____
5	5	_____	3 x 180° = _____
6	_____	_____	_____
7	_____	_____	_____
8	_____	_____	_____
10	_____	_____	_____
N	_____	_____	_____
			Write in the formula.

34

The formula (N - 2) x 180° gives the sum of all the angles for any polygon. We can adapt this formula to find the size of each angle in regular polygons.

Remember, regular polygons have all sides equal and all angles equal. Because all angles are the same measurement, we can take the sum of all the angles and divide it by the number of angles in the polygon.

An example: A regular pentagon has a sum of angles of 540°.

$$(5 - 2) \times 180° = 540°$$

Divide 540° by 5 to get the size of each angle.

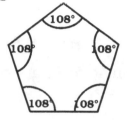

To find the size of each angle in a regular polygon, use the formula: $\frac{(N-2) \times 180°}{N}$.

Fill in the chart for regular polygons.

Number of polygon sides.	Sum of all angles.	Size of each angle.
4	(4 - 2) x 180°= _____	$\frac{360°}{4}$ = _____
5	_____	$\frac{540}{5}$ = _____
6	_____	_____
8	_____	_____
10	_____	_____
N	(N - 2) x 180°	$\frac{(N-2) \times 180°}{N}$

Keep in mind the formula (N - 2) x 180° can be used for all polygons, but the formula $\frac{(N-2) \times 180°}{N}$ is only for regular polygons.

Exterior Angles of Polygons

Exterior angles are formed by extending one end of each polygon side. On any polygon, regular and irregular, there is a relationship with exterior angles. On any polygon, exterior angles will all add up to 360°.

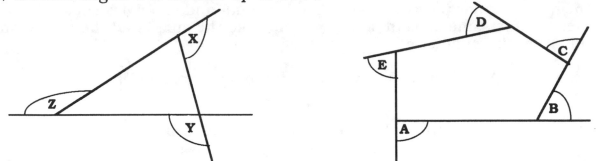

X, Y, and Z are exterior angles.   A, B, C, D, and E are exterior angles.

An angle and its adjacent exterior angle form a straight line or straight angle. The measurement of a straight angle is 180°.

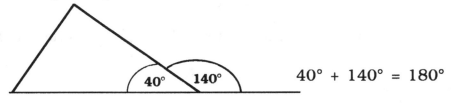

$$40° + 140° = 180°$$

To find the size of an exterior angle, subtract the interior angle size from 180°.

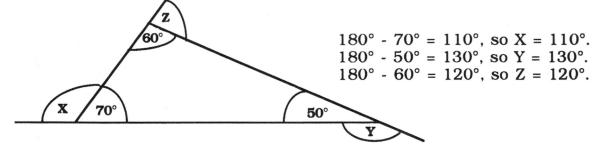

$180° - 70° = 110°$, so X = 110°.
$180° - 50° = 130°$, so Y = 130°.
$180° - 60° = 120°$, so Z = 120°.

Adding up all exterior angles (110° + 130° + 120), we find that the sum of the exterior angles is 360°.

Example 1: Find the size of each exterior angle and add them up.

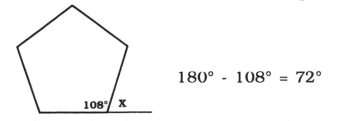

$$180° - 108° = 72°$$

For a regular pentagon there are five exterior angles, each one measures 72°:
5 x 72° = 360°.

Solving the Number of Sides of a Polygon

Given the size of an exterior angle, we can tell how many sides a regular polygon has.

There are two ways to solve for the number of sides.

Method 1
Since the exterior and interior angles sum to 180°, the interior angle is 135° (180° - 45° = 135°). Using the formula for the size of each angle of a regular polygon, we can solve for N.

$$\frac{(N-2)\ 180°}{N} = 135°$$
$$(N - 2)\ 180° = 135N$$
$$180N - 360° = 135N$$
$$45N = 360°$$
$$N = \frac{360}{45}$$
$$N = 8 \text{ sides}$$

Method 2
All the exterior angles will sum to 360°.

$$45N = 360°$$
$$N = \frac{360}{45}$$
$$N = 8 \text{ sides}$$

1. How many sides does the regular polygon have if each exterior angle is 30°?

2. Find the size of each exterior angle and add them up.

A. Square   B. Regular hexagon

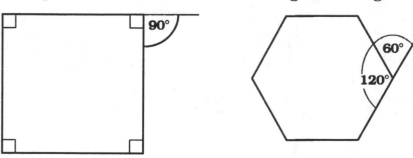

37

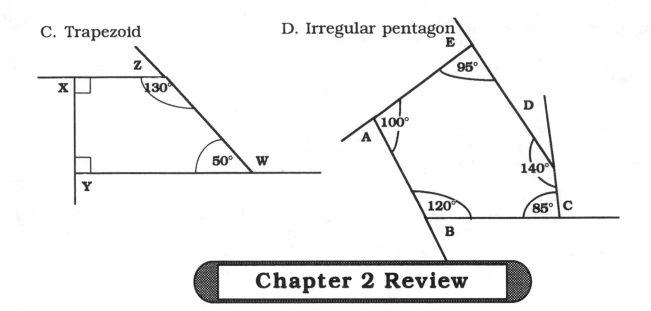

C. Trapezoid

D. Irregular pentagon

Chapter 2 Review

Midpoints of the sides:

The line formed by connecting the midpoints of two sides of a triangle is equal to half of the third side and is parallel to the third side.

On a trapezoid, the median is the line formed by connecting the midpoints of the non-parallel sides. The median is parallel to the parallel sides and equal to half the sum of the two parallel sides.

Isosceles trapezoid:

An isosceles trapezoid has the two non-parallel sides equal and the base angles equal.

Isosceles triangle:

An isosceles triangle has two sides equal and the two angles that are opposite these sides are equal.

Triangle inequality:

The sum of any two sides of a triangle is greater than the third side.

Angles:

The sum of all angles in any polygon can be found using the formula $(N - 2) \, 180°$ where N is the number of sides.

The size of each angle in a regular polygon can be found using the formula $\frac{(N-2) \times 180°}{N}$, where N is the number of sides.

The sum of the exterior angles of any polygon is $360°$.

Properties of quadrilaterals:

	Quadrilateral	Parallelogram	Rectangle	Rhombus	Square	Trapezoids
Opposite sides equal.		●	●	●	●	
Opposite sides parallel.		●	●	●	●	
All sides are equal.				●	●	
Opposite angles equal.		●	●	●	●	
All angles are 90°.			●		●	
Diagonals bisecting.		●	●	●	●	
Diagonals are equal.			●		●	
Diagonals perpendicular.				●	●	

The accompanying diagrams show the relationships between quadrilaterals.

A square is a rectangle
    and a rhombus
    and a parallelogram
    and a quadrilateral.

A rectangle is a parallelogram
    and a quadrilateral,
    but not a square or
    a rhombus.

A rhombus is a parallelogram
    and a quadrilateral,
    but not a square or
    a rectangle.

A parallelogram is a quadrilateral.
It is not necessarily a rhombus,
rectangle, or square, although
it could be.

A trapezoid is a quadrilateral
with only one set of opposite
sides parallel, but it is not a
parallelogram.

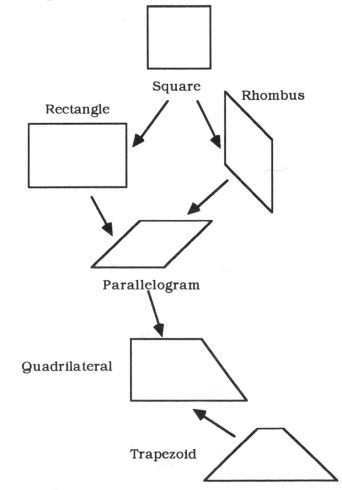

Square

Rhombus

Rectangle

Parallelogram

Quadrilateral

Trapezoid

1. Find the measure of each angle of a regular 20-gon.

2. Given a partial drawing of a regular polygon and some angle measurements, determine how many sides it has.

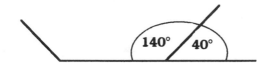

3. How may sides does a regular polygon have if its interior angles are twice the size of its exterior angles?

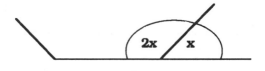

4. After nailing a window casing together, how can Tom be sure it is a rectangular shape if he has only a tape measure to use?

5. To measure across a hole in the ground that is inaccessible to direct measurement, Nikki paced off a triangle on the ground as shown in the diagram. What is the width of the hole? Why?

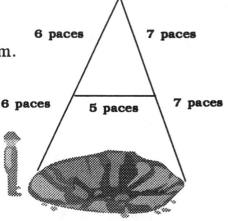

6. If an isosceles triangle has a side of 13 and a side of 27, what is the size of the third side?

7. What is the measurement of EF?

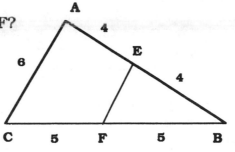

8. What is the measurement of angle X?

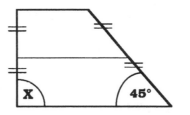

9. Which quadrilaterals are parallelograms? Why? The figures are distorted.

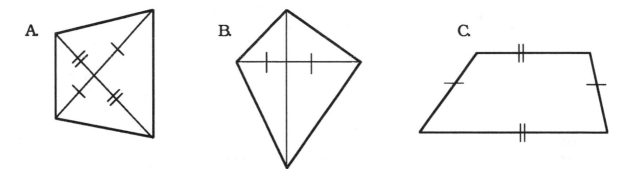

A.

B.

C.

10. Can this quadrilateral have just one 90° angle? What do the other angles measure? What is the most specific name for the figure?

Given AD ‖ CB and AB ‖ DC.

D   C

A   B

Pythagorean Theorem

The Pythagorean Theorem provides a formula that can be used to find the lengths of the legs or the hypotenuse of a right triangle.

The theorem states: The sum of two squared legs ($a^2 + b^2$) is equal to the square of the hypotenuse (c^2).

The formula is: $\mathbf{a^2 + b^2 = c^2}$.

In order to use the formula, a triangle must be a right triangle and two of the sides must be known.

To find the missing <u>hypotenuse</u>, use the given measurements of the legs.

$$12^2 + 4^2 = Y^2$$
$$144 + 16 = Y^2$$
$$160 = Y^2$$
$$\sqrt{160} = Y$$
$$12.65 = Y$$

The hypotenuse measures 12.65 meters.

To find the missing <u>leg</u> use the given measurements of the leg and the hypotenuse.

$$X^2 + 16^2 = 20^2$$
$$X^2 + 256 = 400$$
$$X^2 = 400 - 256$$
$$X^2 = 144$$
$$X = \sqrt{144}$$
$$X = 12$$

The missing leg is 12 meters.

Practice

Solve for the missing side.

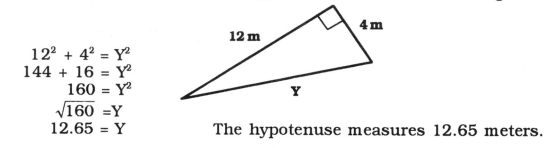

1. 12 m, 5 m, Y

2. 10, 8, X

3. T, 5, 3

42

Converse of the Pythagorean Theorem

We can also use the Pythagorean Theorem to determine if a triangle is a right triangle. For a triangle, if the sum of two squared sides is equal to the square of the third side, then the triangle is a right triangle.

Use the formula to determine if the following triangles are right triangles. The pictures are distorted.

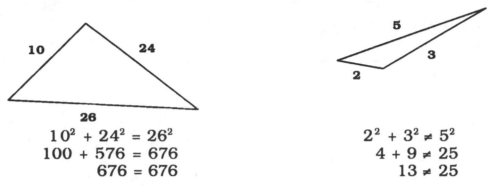

$10^2 + 24^2 = 26^2$
$100 + 576 = 676$
$676 = 676$

$2^2 + 3^2 \neq 5^2$
$4 + 9 \neq 25$
$13 \neq 25$

Yes, this is a right triangle.   No, this is not a right triangle.

Practice

1. If a triangle had sides of 16 cm, 34 cm, and 30 cm, is it a right triangle?

2. If a triangle has sides of 2, 3, and 3, is it a right triangle?

Longest Diagonal of a Rectangular Solid

We can use the Pythagorean Theorem to find the longest diagonal of a rectanglar solid. The longest diagonal is the greatest distance between any two corners of rectangular solid. The Pythagorean Theorem will be used to develop a special formula to find this diagonal.

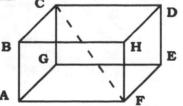

Line segments AD, CF, BE, and GH are all longest diagonals, and they are equal to each other.

Given a box with height of 3, width of 4, and a length of 5, find the longest diagonal AD.

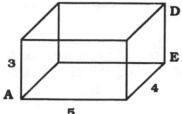

First, find the diagonal AE on the bottom of the box by using the Pythagorean Theorem.

Box bottom.

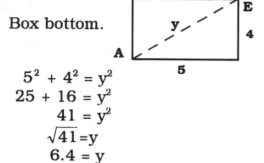

$$5^2 + 4^2 = y^2$$
$$25 + 16 = y^2$$
$$41 = y^2$$
$$\sqrt{41} = y$$
$$6.4 = y$$

Next, find the longest diagonal AD. Notice how the longest diagonal is the hypotenuse of a right triangle formed by the diagonal of the bottom of the box and by the height of the box.

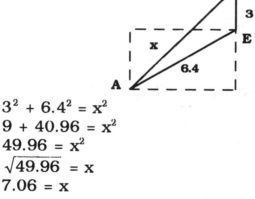

$$3^2 + 6.4^2 = x^2$$
$$9 + 40.96 = x^2$$
$$49.96 = x^2$$
$$\sqrt{49.96} = x$$
$$7.06 = x$$

We used the Pythagorean Theorem twice to find the longest diagonal. This time we will find it using just letters in order to develop the formula.

a = height
b = length
c = width
d = longest diagonal

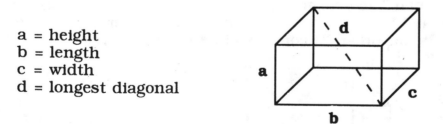

First, use $b^2 + c^2$ to get the diagonal of the bottom.

Then, combine this ($b^2 + c^2$) with the height in the Pythagorean Theorem:

$$(b^2 + c^2) + a^2 = d^2.$$

44

All three dimensions (height, length, and width) of the solid are used. Each one is squared and the three squares are added together. The sum is equal to the square of the longest diagonal. To find the longest diagonal, take the square root of the sum.

For example: If a box has the dimensions of 10, 12, and 14 the longest diagonal would be:

$$d^2 = 10^2 + 12^2 + 14^2$$
$$d^2 = 100 + 144 + 196$$
$$d^2 = 440$$
$$d = \sqrt{440}$$
$$d = 20.97$$

Practice

1. Find the longest diagonal of a rectangular box if the height is 4, the length is 9, and the width is 5.

2. Find the longest diagonal of a box with height of h, width of w, and length of l. Hint: since the dimensions are unknown, put the variables into the formula.

3   Area of an Equilateral Triangle

An equilateral triangle has all three sides equal and all three angles equal. The Pythagorean Theorem can be used to derive a formula to find the area of an equilateral triangle when the height is not known. The formula is $\frac{\sqrt{3}}{4} S^2$. where S is the measurement of the side of the triangle.

Proof: If a triangle is an equilateral triangle, then its area is $\frac{\sqrt{3}}{4} S^2$.

Draw a perpendicular line from a vertex to the middle of the opposite side.

Let CD = h, the unknown height.
CB = S, the hypotenuse of right triangle BDC.
DB = $\frac{1}{2}$S.

45

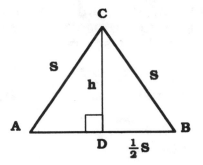

Use the Pythagorean Theorem to find CD (the height of the triangle), then we will find the area.

Solve for h:

$$S^2 = h^2 + (\tfrac{1}{2}S)^2$$
$$S^2 = h^2 + \tfrac{1}{4}S^2$$
$$S^2 - \tfrac{1}{4}S^2 = h^2$$
$$\tfrac{3}{4}S^2 = h^2$$
$$\sqrt{\tfrac{3}{4}S^2} = h$$
$$\tfrac{\sqrt{3}}{2}S = h$$

Now, we can use the formula for the area of any triangle:
$$A = \tfrac{1}{2} \times base \times height.$$
Let the base = S
$$height = \tfrac{\sqrt{3}}{2}S$$

$$Area = \tfrac{1}{2} \times S \times \tfrac{\sqrt{3}}{2}S$$
$$= \tfrac{1}{2} \times \tfrac{\sqrt{3}}{2}S^2$$
$$= \tfrac{\sqrt{3}}{4}S^2$$

So the formula for the area of an equilateral triangle is:

$$A = \tfrac{\sqrt{3}}{4}S^2$$

For example: Find the area of an equilateral triangle with all sides equal to 6 cm.

Use the formula: $A = \tfrac{\sqrt{3}}{4}S^2$

$$A = \frac{\sqrt{3}}{4} S^2$$

$$A = \frac{\sqrt{3}}{4} (6^2)$$

$$A = \frac{\sqrt{3}}{4} (36)$$

$$A = \sqrt{3} (9)$$

$$A = 15.59 \text{ cm}^2$$

Find the area of each triangle.

1.

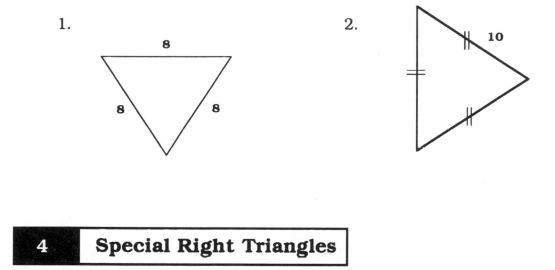

2.

---

4   Special Right Triangles

The Pythagorean Theorem can be used to find constant relationships between the sides of right triangles. The 45°–45°–90° and 30°–60°–90° triangles occur often and are used in trigonometry.

45°–45°–90° Triangles

If a right triangle has two angles equal, then it is an isosceles right triangle and two legs are equal in length.

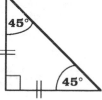

Given the measurement of the legs, the Pythagorean Theorem can be used to find the hypotenuse.

$$8^2 + 8^2 = h^2$$
$$64 + 64 = h^2$$
$$128 = h^2$$
$$\sqrt{128} = h$$
$$\sqrt{64 \cdot 2} = h$$
$$\sqrt{64} \cdot \sqrt{2} = h$$
$$8\sqrt{2} = h$$

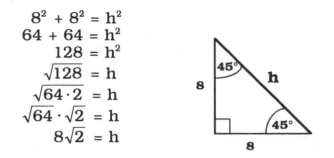

Notice how the hypotenuse is $\sqrt{2}$ times the measurement of a leg. This is a constant relationship between the legs and the hypotenuse of a 45°–45°–90° triangle.

$$L^2 + L^2 = h^2$$
$$2L^2 = h^2$$
$$\sqrt{2L^2} = h$$
$$L\sqrt{2} = h$$

If we know the hypotenuse, we can find the size of the legs. To do so, we can use the Pythagorean Theorem or the constant relationship.

$$y^2 + y^2 = 12^2$$
$$2y^2 = 144$$
$$y^2 = \frac{144}{2}$$
$$y^2 = 72$$
$$y = \sqrt{72}$$
$$y = 8.48$$

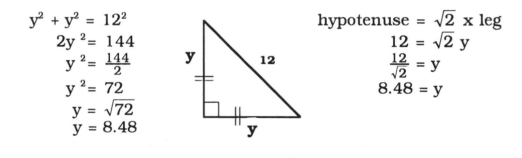

$$\text{hypotenuse} = \sqrt{2} \times \text{leg}$$
$$12 = \sqrt{2}\, y$$
$$\frac{12}{\sqrt{2}} = y$$
$$8.48 = y$$

Practice

1. Find the hypotenuse of a 45°–45°–90° triangle if the legs are 10 cm.

2. If the hypotenuse is 20 meters on an isosceles right triangle, find the measurements of the legs.

30°–60°–90° Triangles

The Pythagorean Theorem shows a constant relationship between the sides of a 30°–60°–90° triangle.

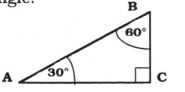

Notice how two of these triangles can be put together to form an equilateral triangle.

On the original triangle ABC, side BC is opposite the 30° angle. Side BC is half the size of BB¹ on the equilateral triangle. Since all sides are equal on the equilateral triangle:

$$BC = \frac{1}{2}BB^1 \quad \text{and} \quad BC = \frac{1}{2}AB.$$

AB is the hypotenuse of the original triangle ABC. In any 30°–60°–90° triangle, the short leg opposite the 30° angle has half the size of the hypotenuse.

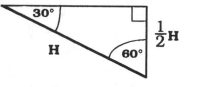

Given two sides of a right triangle, we can use the Pythagorean Theorem to find the third side and to discover another constant relationship.

Solve for L:
$$L^2 + \left(\frac{1}{2}H\right)^2 = H^2$$
$$L^2 + \frac{1}{4}H^2 = H^2$$
$$L^2 = H^2 - \frac{1}{4}H^2$$
$$L^2 = \frac{3}{4}H^2$$
$$L = \sqrt{\frac{3}{4}H^2}$$
$$L = \frac{\sqrt{3}}{2}H$$

In any 30°–60°–90° triangle, the long leg is $\frac{\sqrt{3}}{2}$x hypotenuse.

•For Example: Find the missing legs.

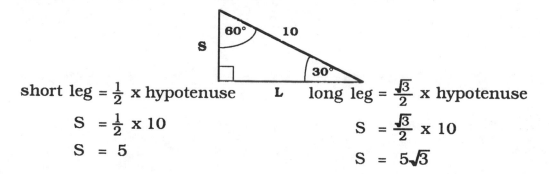

short leg = $\frac{1}{2}$ x hypotenuse

$S = \frac{1}{2}$ x 10

$S = 5$

long leg = $\frac{\sqrt{3}}{2}$ x hypotenuse

$S = \frac{\sqrt{3}}{2}$ x 10

$S = 5\sqrt{3}$

•Another Example: Given the short leg, find the hypotenuse and the long leg.

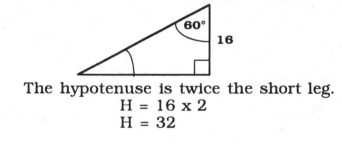

The hypotenuse is twice the short leg.
$$H = 16 \times 2$$
$$H = 32$$

The long leg is $\frac{\sqrt{3}}{2}$ times the hypotenuse.
$$L = \frac{\sqrt{3}}{2} \times 32$$
$$L = 16\sqrt{3}$$

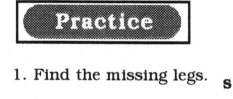

Practice

1. Find the missing legs.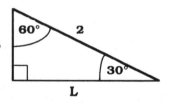

2. Find the missing hypotenuse and leg.

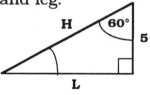

The Pythagorean Theorem can be used to find the measurements of the sides of a right triangle. The theorem states that the square of the hypotenuse is equal to the sum of the squares of the other two legs.

The formula is $a^2 + b^2 = c^2$, where c is the hypotenuse and a and b are the legs.

Converse of the Pythagorean Theorem:

If the sum of the squares of two sides of a triangle equals the square of the third side, then the triangle is a right triangle.

Longest Diagonal of a Rectangular Solid:

The three dimensions of a rectangular solid (height, length, and width) can be used to find the length of the longest diagonal.

$$d = \sqrt{l^2 + w^2 + h^2}$$

Where d is the longest diagonal
l is the length of the rectangular solid
w is the width of the rectangular solid
h is the height of the rectangular solid

Area of an Equilateral Triangle:

The formula for the area of an equilateral triangle is:

$$A = \frac{\sqrt{3}}{4}S^2$$

Where S is the measurement of the side.

45°–45°–90° Triangle:

The constant relationship between the sides of an isosceles right triangle is:

the hypotenuse is $\sqrt{2}$ times the leg.

30°–60°–90° Triangle:

The constant relationships between the sides of 30°–60° right triangles are:

the short leg is half the hypotenuse,
The long leg is $\frac{\sqrt{3}}{2}$ times the hypotenuse.

1. Find the length of each side of the square. (Hint: what kind of triangle is formed by the diagonal of the square?)

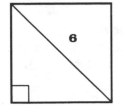

2. Can a triangle with sides of 4, 4, and 6 be a right triangle?

3. A truck is driven seven miles due north and then six miles due east. What is the distance between the starting and ending points? (Hint: draw a picture.)

4. Find the length of the hypotenuse and the long leg of a right triangle that has a 30° angle and a short leg of 8 inches.

5. Will Ruthie be able to pack her 26-inch baton into a suitcase that measures 8 inches by 14 inches by 20 inches?

6. A baseball diamond is a square with sides of 90 feet. When the third baseman throws the ball from third base to first base, how far does the ball travel?

7. An antenna is to be erected perpendicularly to a roof. A guy wire will be attached 7 feet from the base of the antenna. At the top of the antenna, the guy wire will form a 60° angle. How long should the guy wire be?

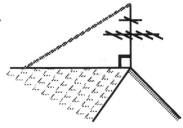

8. A skateboard ramp is inclined 30° up from the ground. If you move 15 feet up the ramp, how high above the ground are you?

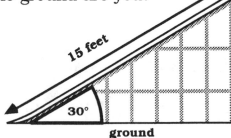

9. A fence is to be built from a corner of one square field to the opposite corner. If each side of the field measures 30 yards, how long is the fence?

10. A tent is formed like a pyramid with a floor in the shape of an equilateral triangle measuring 10 feet on each side. If the floor is to be covered with a tarp, how many square feet of tarp would be needed?

Measurement
Perimeter • Area • Volume

Measurements can be made on figures and solids. Specific units are used for each type of measurement.

Perimeter is measured in units such as centimeter, meter, inch, feet, etc.

Area is measured in **square units** such as square centimeters, square meters, square inches, square feet, etc.

Volume is measured in **cubic units** such as cubic centimeters, cubic meters, cubic inches, cubic feet, etc.

1   Perimeter

Perimeter is the distance around a figure. For polygons, the perimeter is the sum of the lengths of all sides.

Irregular Polygons

The perimeter of this pentagon is the sum of all the sides:

$$P = 5 + 3 + 4 + 3 + 4 = 19$$

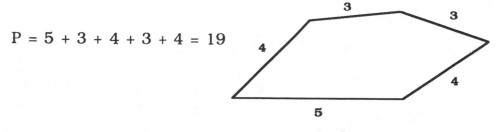

Squares

The perimeter of a square can be found by using the formula P= 4 x S, where S is the length of each side.

P = 4 x 8
P = 32

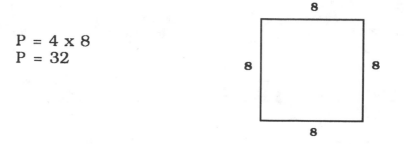

Rectangles

The perimeter of a rectangle can be found using the formula P = 2L + 2W, where L is the length and W is the width.

P = 2 x 8 + 2 x 4
P = 16 + 8 = 24

Notice how the sides of a polygon can be redrawn into a line (using the rectangle as an example):

| 4 | 8 | 4 | 8 |

The perimeter is the sum of a figure's line segments; thus, it is a linear measurement.

Circles

The distance around a circle is also a linear measurement called circumference.

The circumference is found by using the constant relationship between the circumference and the diameter. In all circles, the ratio of circumference to diameter is approximately 3.14 or π (pronounced *pi*).

Since $\frac{C}{D} = \pi$, then circumference equals the diameter times π.

$\frac{C}{D} = \pi$ $\qquad$ C = Dπ $\qquad$ or $\qquad$ C = 2πR as the diameter is twice the radius.

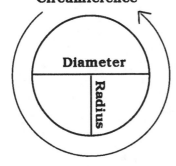

Example: Find the circumference of this circle.

C = Dπ
C = 12π
C = 12 x 3.14 = 37.68

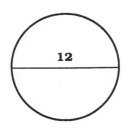

Find the perimeter or circumference of each figure.

1.

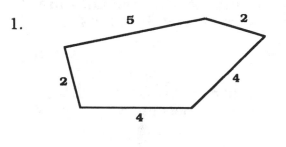

2.

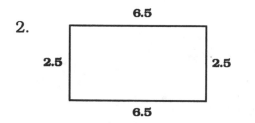

3.

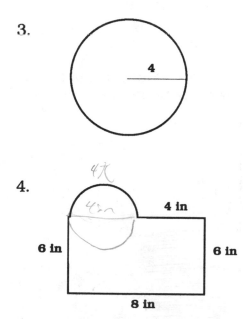

4.

5. Find the perimeter of a rhombus with a side length of 3.25 feet.

To measure the region within a figure, we use square units. In polygons, two dimensions (sides) are multiplied to gain the square units. The two sides are perpendicular to each other. Some polygons have specific area formulas.

Rectangles

To count the square units in a rectangle, multiply the two perpendicular sides called the length and width. The area formula becomes: A = L x W.

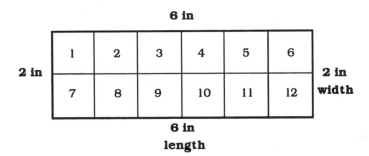

A = 2 x 6 = 12 square inches.

Squares

A square is a special rectangle with all four sides equal. The formula is the same as the area of a rectangle except that S is used for both sides: A = S x S or A= S^2.

1	2	3	4	5
6	7	8	9	10
11	12	13	14	15
16	17	18	19	20
21	22	23	24	25

5 m

5m

A = 5 x 5 = 25 square meters.

Parallelograms

A parallelogram can be rearranged to form a rectangle with a side perpendicular to the base. The area formula is the same as the rectangle but the letters B and H are used for base and height: A = B x H.

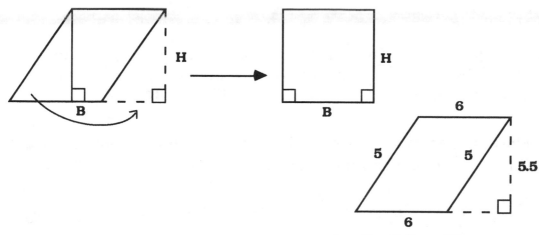

A = 6 x 5.5 = 33 square units.
Be careful not to use 6 x 5 as
those sides are not perpendicular
to each other.

Triangles

With any triangle, two congruent copies can be put together to form a
parallelogram. The area of the parallelogram is base times height, but
since the triangle is only half the area of the parallelogram, the area
formula for a triangle becomes: $A = \frac{1}{2} \times B \times H$.

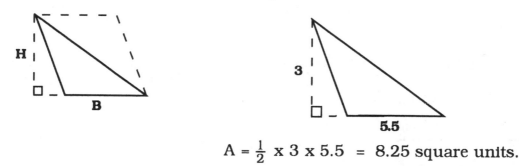

$A = \frac{1}{2} \times 3 \times 5.5 = 8.25$ square units.

Trapezoids

With any trapezoid two congruent copies can form a parallelogram. The base
of the parallelogram results from combining the two parallel sides of the
trapezoid. In the area formula, the base is written as (a + b). Since the
trapezoid is only half of the parallelogram, the area formula for a trapezoid
becomes: $A = \frac{1}{2} \times H \times (a + b)$.

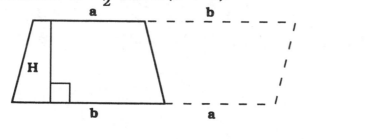

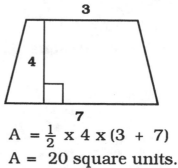

$A = \frac{1}{2} \times 4 \times (3 + 7)$
$A = 20$ square units.

Circles

The area of a circle is measured in square units. A circle can be cut in half (Fig. 1), and each half can be further divided so that the resulting parts fit together to form a parallelogram (Fig. 2 yields Fig. 3). In that parallelogram, the base is $\frac{1}{2}$ of the circumference and the height is the radius. The formula B x H becomes $\frac{1}{2}$ x C x R or $\frac{1}{2}$ x 2πR x R which simplifies to πR². Thus, the area formula for a circle is: $A = \pi R^2$

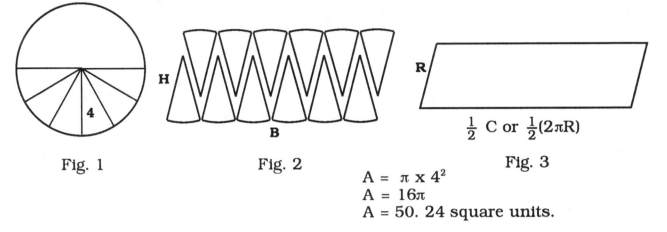

H

B

Fig. 1

Fig. 2

R

$\frac{1}{2}$ C or $\frac{1}{2}(2\pi R)$

Fig. 3

$A = \pi \times 4^2$
$A = 16\pi$
$A = 50.\ 24$ square units.

Irregular Shapes

The area of irregular shapes can be found by dividing them into smaller shapes that have area formulas, determining the areas of those shapes, and then adding all areas together.

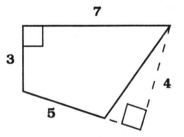

This shape can be divided into two triangles. The area of triangle I is : $A = \frac{1}{2}$ x 3 x 7 = 10.5 square units.

The area of triangle II is :
  $A = \frac{1}{2}$ x 5 x 4 = 10 square units.

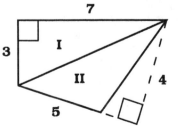

The total area is 20.5 square units.

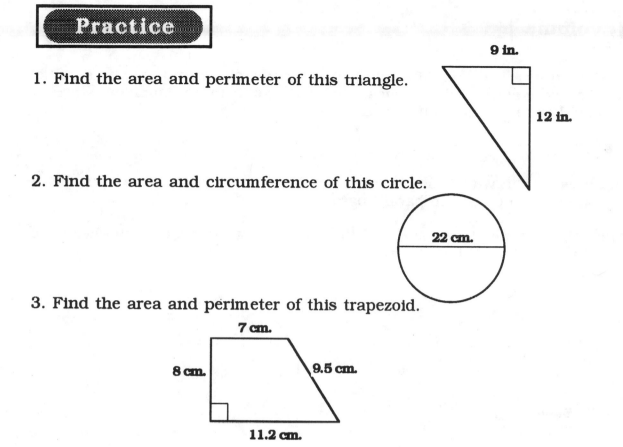

1. Find the area and perimeter of this triangle.

9 in.

12 in.

2. Find the area and circumference of this circle.

22 cm.

3. Find the area and perimeter of this trapezoid.

7 cm.

8 cm.   9.5 cm.

11.2 cm.

4. Find the area and perimeter of a 3-inch by 5-inch photograph.

5. Find the area and perimeter of this irregular figure.

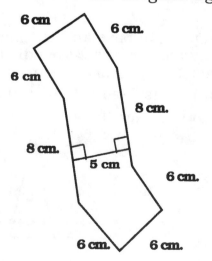

6 cm   6 cm.

6 cm

8 cm.

8 cm.

5 cm   6 cm.

6 cm.   6 cm.

3   Volume

To measure the interior regions of solid shapes, we use cubic units such as cubic centimeters, cubic meters, cubic inches, etc. In a solid, three dimensions are multiplied together to gain the cubic units.

Prisms

A prism is a solid with bases that are congruent polygons that are parallel to each other. The sides are parallelograms.

To find the volume of a prism, multiply the area of the base by the height of the solid: V = (area of base) x H.

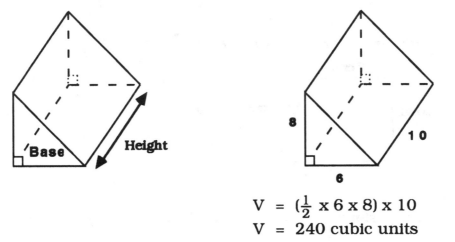

$$V = (\tfrac{1}{2} \times 6 \times 8) \times 10$$
$$V = 240 \text{ cubic units}$$

Pyramids

A pyramid is a solid with a polygon base and triangular sides that meet at a point. The height of a pyramid is the perpendicular distance from the base to the point. Since three pyramids can fit together to form a prism, the volume formula results from taking $\frac{1}{3}$ the volume of the related prism. The formula for the volume of a pyramid is:
$$V = \tfrac{1}{3} \times \text{height} \times \text{area of base}.$$

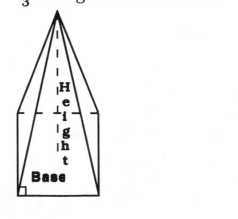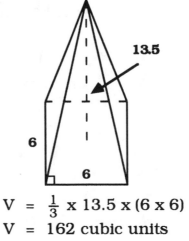

$$V = \tfrac{1}{3} \times 13.5 \times (6 \times 6)$$
$$V = 162 \text{ cubic units}$$

60

Cones

A cone resembles a pyramid except that its sides are curved and its base is usually circular. Its volume formula resembles the volume formula for a pyramid: $V = \frac{1}{3}$ x height x area of base. Since the base is a circle, the formula becomes: $V = \frac{1}{3}$ x h x πr^2. The height (h) is perpendicular to the radius (r).

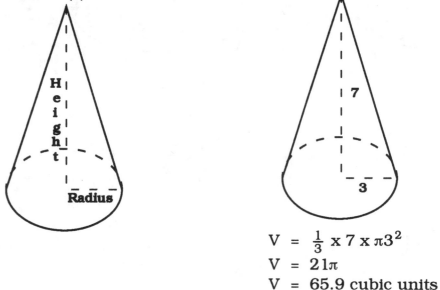

$V = \frac{1}{3} \times 7 \times \pi 3^2$

$V = 21\pi$

$V = 65.9$ cubic units

Cylinders

A cylinder resembles a prism except that its sides are curved and its base is usually circular. Its volume formula resembles the volume formula of a prism: V = height x area of base. Since the base of a cyclinder is circular, the formula becomes: $V = h \times \pi r^2$.

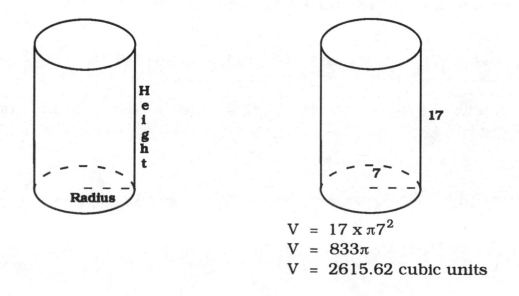

$V = 17 \times \pi 7^2$

$V = 833\pi$

$V = 2615.62$ cubic units

61

Spheres

A sphere is a three dimensional round shape. Its volume is also measured in cubic units using the formula: $V = \frac{4}{3} \times \pi\, r^3$.

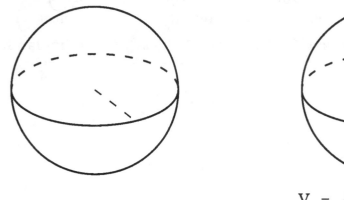 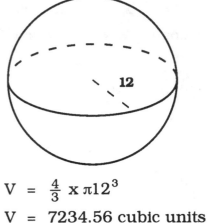

$$V = \frac{4}{3} \times \pi 12^3$$
$$V = 7234.56 \text{ cubic units}$$

Practice

1. Find the volume of a pyramid with a base area of 24 square inches and a height of 9 inches.

2. Find the volume of a rectangular solid with the dimensions of: length = 3 cm, width = 4 cm, and height = 6 cm.

3. Find the volume of a sphere with a diameter of 10 yards.

4. Find the volume of a cone that is 5 inches tall and has a diameter of 3 inches.

5. Find the volume of a cylindrical glass that is 3 inches high and with a diameter of 2.5 inches.

Perimeter is the distance around a figure and is measured in units.

Perimeter of a square:	$P = 4S$
Perimeter of a rectangle:	$P = 2L + 2W$
Perimeter of a circle:	$C = 2\pi r$ or $C = D\pi$

Area is the interior region of a flat figure and is measured in square units.

Area of a rectangle:	$A = LW$
Area of a square:	$A = S^2$
Area of a parallelogram:	$A = BH$
Area of a triangle:	$A = \frac{1}{2} BH$
Area of a trapezoid:	$A = \frac{1}{2}H(a + b)$
Area of a circle:	$A = \pi r^2$

Volume is the capacity of solids and is measured in cubic units.

Volume of a prism:	$V = H \times$ (area of base)
Volume of a pyramid:	$V = \frac{1}{3} \times H \times$ (area of base)
Volume of a cone:	$V = \frac{1}{3} \times H \times \pi r^2$
Volume of a cylinder:	$V = H \times \pi r^2$
Volume of a sphere:	$V = \frac{4}{3}\pi r^3$

1. Find the perimeter and area of a sheet of paper that measures 8.5 inches by 11 inches.

2. If a square has a perimeter of 28 meters, what is its area?

3. How much will it cost to carpet a 15 feet by 15 feet room if the carpet costs $5.95 per square foot?

4. Find the perimeter of this figure:

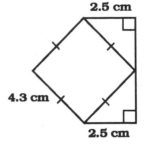

5. Find the volume of an enclosed phone booth that is 8 feet high and has a square floor with a side of 3 feet.

6. Find the volume of a cylinder with a height of 6 inches and a base circumference of 14 inches.

7. Find the volume of this container:

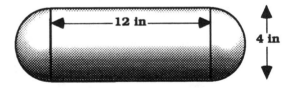

8. If a circular fish pond is 8.5 meters across, what is the area of the top surface and what is the distance around it?

9. Loretta's perfume bottle is in the shape of a pyramid with an equilateral triangle for a base. The sides of the triangle measure 2 inches each and the bottle is 4.5 inches tall. How many cubic inches does the bottle hold?

10. Find the volume of a prism that is 18 centimeters tall with trapezoid bases that resembles this figure:

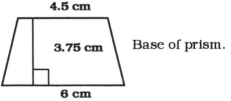

Base of prism.

Similar figures are figures that have the same shape but are different sizes. The corresponding angles of similar figures are equal but the corresponding linear dimensions are different.

The symbol or notation for similarity is $\sim$. Similar figures can be used to find or predict missing measurements.

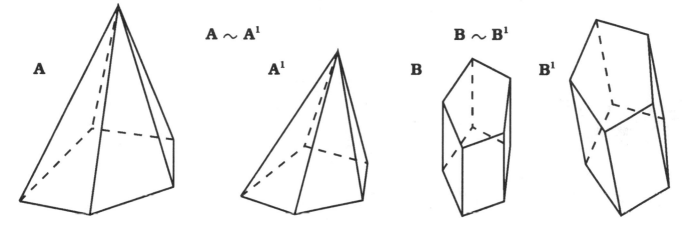

On the similar polygons below, notice that the corresponding angles are equal while the length of the corresponding sides have all been increased two times. The amount that changes the linear dimensions is called the **scaling factor**. Given similar figures, we can find the scaling factor by setting up the ratios of the corresponding sides.

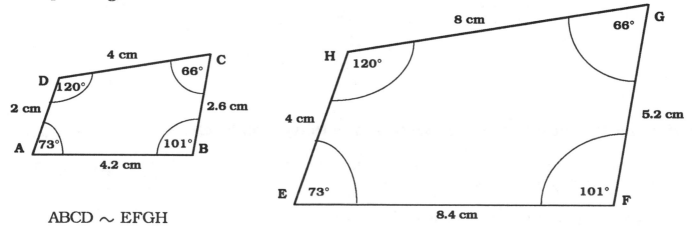

ABCD $\sim$ EFGH

In the quadrilaterals above, the scaling factor of the large quadrilateral to the small quadrilateral is 2 to 1 or $\frac{2}{1}$. This ratio is also the ratio of the corresponding sides:

$$\frac{EF}{AB} = \frac{8.4}{4.2} \qquad \frac{FG}{BC} = \frac{5.2}{2.6} \qquad \frac{GH}{CD} = \frac{8}{4} \qquad \frac{HE}{DA} = \frac{4}{2}$$

For example: Find the scaling factor of the figure on the right to the similar figure on the left.

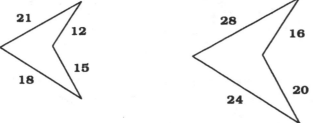

Set up a ratio of corresponding sides and simplify:

$$\frac{\text{right figure}}{\text{left figure}} = \frac{28}{21} = \frac{20}{15} = \frac{16}{12} = \frac{24}{18}$$

Each of the ratios simplifies to $\frac{4}{3}$ or $1\frac{1}{3}$ or $1.\overline{3}$.

Use the sides of these similar figures to find the scale factor of the figure on the right to the figure on the left.

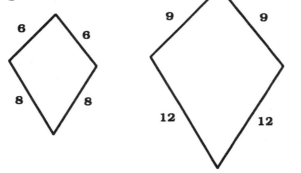

In order for figures to be similar, two conditions must be checked:

1. All corresponding linear dimensions must be proportional; that is, changed by the same scaling factor.

2. All corresponding angles must be equal.

In determining similarity of triangles, however, both conditions need not be checked. There are three short-cuts, or properties, that guarantee similarity in triangles.

If two triangles have all three corresponding angles equal, we can know that they are similar without checking that the corresponding sides are proportional.

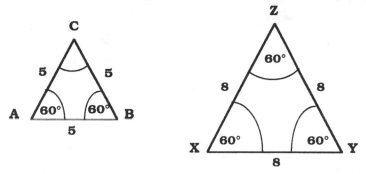

Given that the corresponding angles are equal, $\triangle ABC \sim \triangle XYZ$ by AAA, we can conclude that the corresponding sides are proportional.

Practice

Determine if the two triangles are similar. If they are, find the scaling factor of the triangle on the right to the triangle on the left.

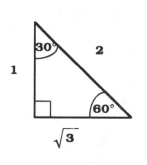

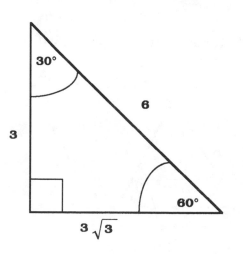

If two triangles have all corresponding sides proportional, then we know that they are similar without checking that the corresponding angles are equal.

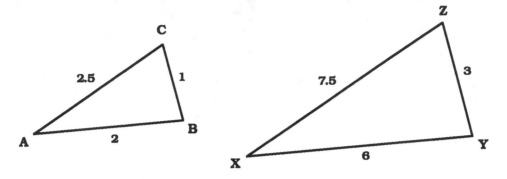

Given that the corresponding sides are proportional:

$$\frac{3}{1} = \frac{6}{2} = \frac{7.5}{2.5}$$

$\triangle ABC \sim \triangle XYZ$ by SSS. We can conclude that the corresponding angles are equal.

Practice

Determine if these triangles are similar. If they are, find the measure of angle Y.

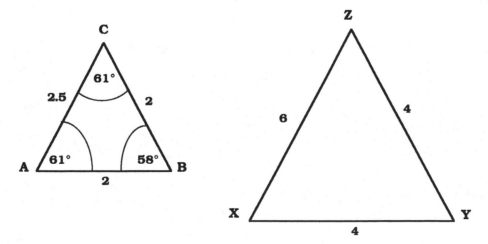

68

If two triangles have two pairs of corresponding sides proportional and equal corresponding angles between these sides, then the triangles are similar.

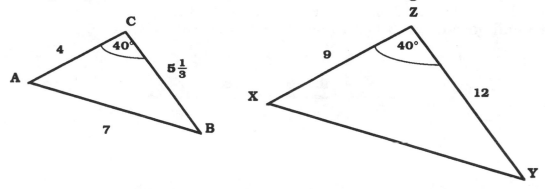

Given that two pairs of corresponding sides are proportional ($\frac{9}{4} = \frac{12}{5.3}$) and given that the included angles are equal ($\angle C = \angle Z$), then $\triangle ABC \sim \triangle XYZ$ by SAS.

We can also conclude that the other corresponding angles are equal and that the other corresponding sides are proportional.

Now that we know that the triangles are similar and that the scaling factor is $\frac{9}{4}$, we can find the missing side XY.

The ratio of $\frac{XY}{AB}$ will also equal the scaling factor.

Given $\overline{AB} = 7$, let $\overline{XY} = n$ $\frac{n}{7} = \frac{9}{4}$.

N can be found by cross multiplying the ratio:

$$7 \times 9 = 4 \times n$$
$$63 = 4n$$
$$\frac{63}{4} = n$$

15.75 = n   Side $\overline{XY}$ = 15.75 units

Determine if the triangles are similar.
If they are, find side XY.

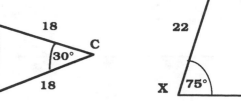

Applications

1. The movement of two people on a seesaw can be shown with similar triangles.

   Marshall sits 150 cm from the center fulcrum and Thomas sits 100 cm from it. If Marshall goes down 30 cm, how far up does Thomas move?

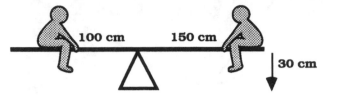

2. Is △UTV∼△STR? If so, find Y.

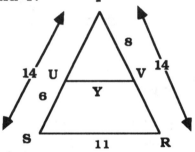

3. Find three triangles in this picture and state what property guarantees that they are similar.

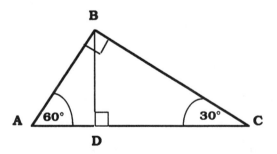

4. State the similarity property of these triangles and find the measurement of X and Y.

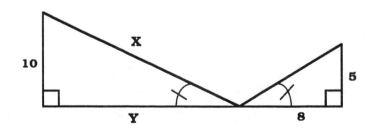

Similarity and the scaling factors can be used to find information about perimeters, areas, and volumes.

Perimeter

Perimeter is a linear dimension. In similar figures, the scaling factor of the sides is the same as the scaling factor of the perimeters. That is, the ratio of the perimeters is the same as the ratio of corresponding sides.

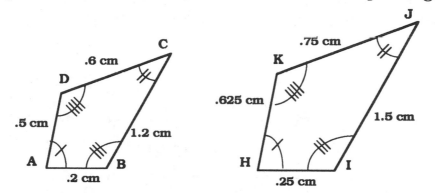

ABCD~HIJK because all corresponding angles are equal and all corresponding sides are proportional:

$$\frac{.25}{.2} = \frac{.625}{.5} = \frac{.75}{.6} = \frac{1.5}{1.2}$$

These ratios all simplify to $\frac{5}{4}$ or 1.25. The perimeter of ABCD is 2.5 cm. The perimeter of HIJK is 3.125 cm. The perimeter ratio of the polygon on the right to the polygon on the left is $\frac{3.125}{2.5}$ which simplifies to $\frac{5}{4}$ or 1.25.

Practice

Check that the ratio of perimeters is the same as the scaling factor of the sides on these similar triangles.

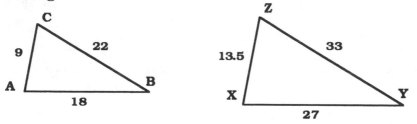

Area

Area is a measurement of squared units resulting from the multiplication of two linear dimensions. With similar figures the ratio of areas is equal to the square of the scaling factor.

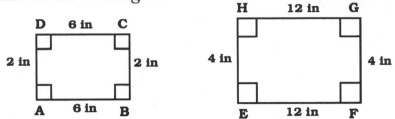

ABCD∽EFGH because the corresponding angles are equal and the corresponding sides are proportional.

$$\frac{12}{6} = \frac{4}{2}$$

The scaling factor is $\frac{2}{1}$. The area of ABCD is 12 square inches and the area of EFGH is 48 square inches. The ratio of these areas is $\frac{48}{12}$ which simplifies to $\frac{4}{1}$ or 4:1. This is also the square of the scaling factor $(\frac{2}{1})^2 = \frac{4}{1}$.

Practice

For these similar triangles, find the scaling factor, the ratio of perimeters, and the ratios of areas.

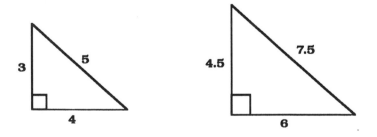

Volume

Volume is a measurement of cubic units resulting from the multiplication of three linear dimensions. With similar figures, the ratio of volume is equal to the cube of the scaling factor.

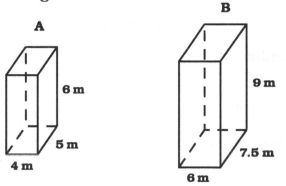

A $\sim$ B. The scaling factor is $\frac{3}{2}$ because the ratio of corresponding sides simplifies to $\frac{3}{2}$.

$$\frac{9}{6} = \frac{7.5}{5} = \frac{6}{4} = \frac{3}{2} = 1.5$$

The volume of A is 4 x 5 x 6 = 120 m³. The volume of B is 6 x 7.5 x 9 = 405 m³. The ratio of volumes is $\frac{405}{120}$ which simplifies to $\frac{27}{8}$ or 3.375. This is the cube of the scaling factor.

$$(1.5)^3 = 3.375$$

Practice

Determine the ratio of volumes for these similar cubes.

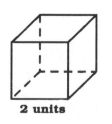

2 units

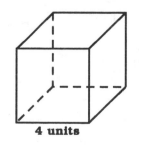

4 units

Similar figures have the same shape but different size. Their corresponding angles are equal and their corresponding sides are proportional.

The scaling factor is the ratio of corresponding sides.

The symbol $\sim$ means similar.

Similar properties of triangles are

AAA	All three corresponding angles equal.
SSS	All three corresponding sides are proportional.
SAS	Two corresponding sides are proportional and the included corresponding angles are equal.

The ratio of perimeters of similar figures equals the scaling factor.

The ratio of areas of similar figures equals the square of the scaling factor.

The ratio of volumes of similar figures equals the cube of the scaling factor.

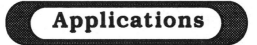

Applications

1. Find the missing sides of the large similar irregular pentagon by finding the scaling factor.

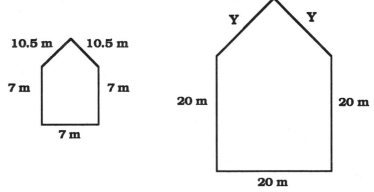

2. Find the perimeters of both pentagons in Problem 1 and show that the ratio of perimeter is the same as the scaling factor.

3. Find the area of the large similar trapezoid given that the linear dimensions are double the small trapezoid and given that the area of the small trapezoid is 5 square meters.

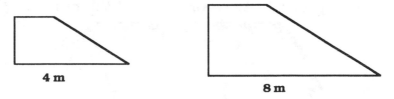

4 m

8 m

4. A small cylindrical can holds 75.36 cubic inches. How much more will a larger, similar cylinder hold if the linear dimensions are increased three times?

5. Given the adjacent diagram, determine how far the external part of a fly's wing moves down if the internal part of the wing moves up 1.36 millimeters.

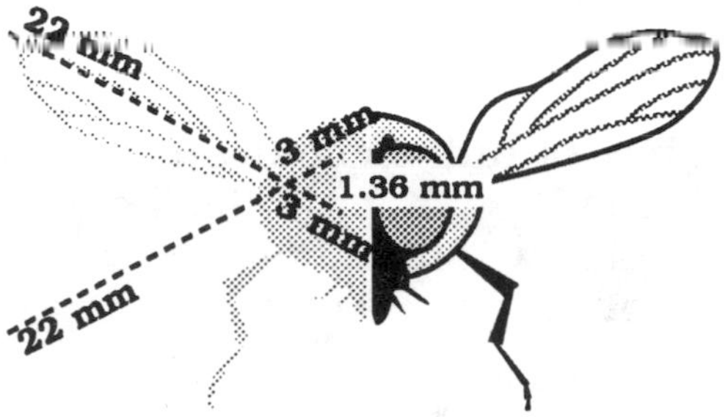

22 mm

3 mm

3 mm

1.36 mm

22 mm

6. Alex uses a crowbar to lift a heavy box. If Alex pushes the end of the bar down 4 feet, how far is the box lifted? (Hint: to see the similar triangles, draw a picture after Alex pushes the end down.)

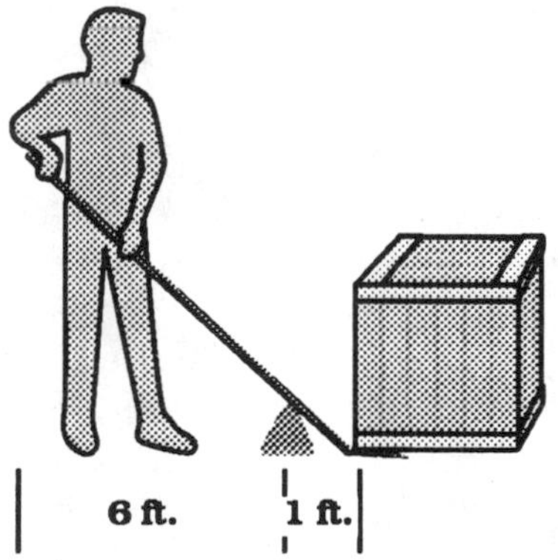

6 ft.   1 ft.

7. After building a garage, Robin decided to build a dog house that was similar to the garage but with the linear dimensions reduced by $2\frac{1}{3}$ times. If the door on the garage is 7 feet high, how high will the door be on the dog house?

8. A sketch for a bulletin board presentation was made on 80 square inches of paper. If the presentation is to be increased by 3 times for placement on a similar bulletin board, how much bulletin board area will be needed?

9. At the hardware store, Chris remembered that he wanted to buy a metal brace for the end of a swing set. He knew the set had 6-foot legs and that the legs were 5 feet apart. At the store, he drew a sketch and decided to attach the brace 4 feet from the ground. How long should the brace be?

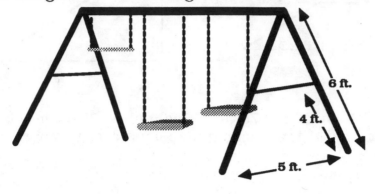

10. A box of fudge cookies measures 4 inches by 6.5 inches by 1.5 inches. It holds 30 cookies. If a similar box is made with all dimensions doubled, how many cookies would it hold?

Final Assessment Test

1. What is the most specific name of each figure? (The drawings may be distorted.)

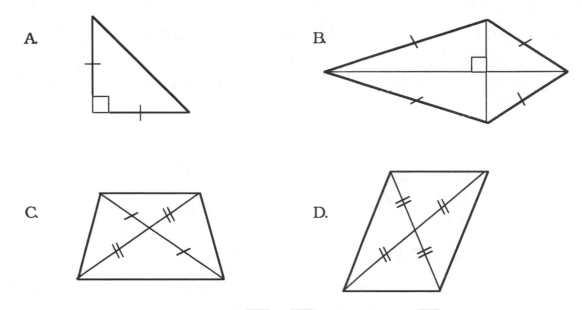

A.

B.

C.

D.

2. Given a rectangular solid with $\overline{AB} = \overline{BC} = 5$ cm and $\overline{CD} = 7$ cm, find the volume and find the longest diagonal $\overline{AD}$.

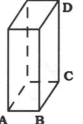

3. For each of the following figures, find the value of x.

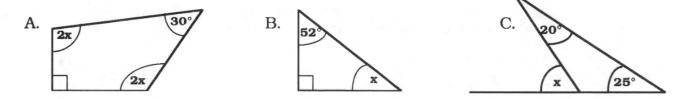

A.   B.   C.

4. A right triangle has a hypotenuse of 11 meters and a leg of 9 meters. Find its area.

5. Decide if the following statements are true or false.

    A. T or F   A parallelogram is a quadrilateral whose opposite sides are parallel.

    B. T or F   A rectangle is a square.

    C. T or F   The diagonals of a rhombus are equal in length.

    D. T or F   On any right triangle, the short leg is half of the hypotenuse.

6. Find the area of $\triangle ABC$ by finding the area of $\triangle ABD$ plus the area of $\triangle CBD$. (Hint: Use the Pythagorean Theorem to find the height of the two triangles.)

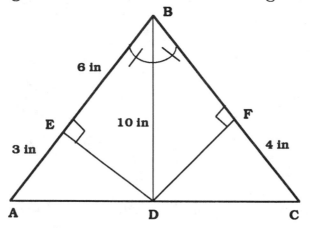

7. Given the rhombus, find the area by first finding the height using the right triangle formed.

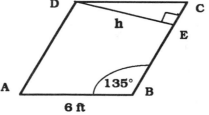

8. Find the area and perimeter of this isosceles trapezoid.

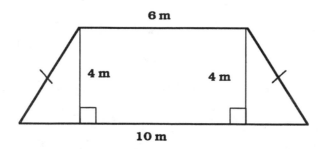

78

Answers

Chapter 1: Congruent Figures

Practice, page 2.
1. Corresponding sides are:

    $\overline{AB} - \overline{ZW} - 4$ centimeters.

    $\overline{BC} - \overline{WX}$ - because both have 2 dashes.

    $\overline{DC} - \overline{YX} - 3.9$ centimeters.

    $\overline{AD} - \overline{ZY} - 2.7$ centimeters.

    Corresponding angles are:

    angle D = angle Y = 105°

    angle B = angle W = 77°

    angle C = angle X because each has 2 dashes.

    angle A = angle Z because each has one dash.

2. 1. Angle D = angle T = 153°

    2. Angle VWY = angle FGI = 42°

    3. Angle RZS = angle BJC = 90°

    4. Line segment GH = WX = 1.2cm.

    5. Line segment TU = DE = 1.5 cm.

Practice, page 4.

$\overline{VO} - \overline{MO}$ and $\overline{VT} - \overline{MT}$ because they are marked with an equal number of dashes. Also both triangles share the same side, so the triangles are congruent by SSS.

∠OTM = ∠OTV = 51° as corresponding angles.

∠TOM = ∠TOV = 54° as corresponding angles.

∠TVO = ∠TMO = 77° They are corresponding angles. Given the size of two angles, the third angle can be found by subtracting the two given sizes from 180°: 180° - 54° - 31° = 75°.

Practice, page 5.

No, we can't be sure they are congruent. There are corresponding equal sides given ($\overline{PT} = \overline{RC}$ and $\overline{AT} = \overline{IC}$); but in order for the triangles to be congruent, the equal angles must be between the given equal corresponding sides. ∠I is not between $\overline{RC}$ and $\overline{CI}$.

If the triangles were marked as:

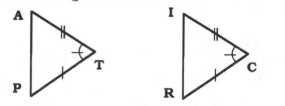

then we could conclude they are congruent by SAS.

Practice, page 7.
1. Yes, the triangles are congruent. Given the size of two angles, we can find the size of the third angles.

ΔABC has angles of 55° and 65°, so ∠C = 60°.

Δ DEF has angles of 60° and 55°, so ∠E = 65°.

Since ∠C = 60° = ∠D and ∠A = ∠F = 55° and $\overline{AC} = \overline{DF}$, then ΔABC ≅ DEF by ASA..

Equal corresponding parts are:

$\overline{AC} = \overline{DF} = 14$ feet.

$\overline{BC} = \overline{DE} = 17$ feet.

$\overline{EF} = \overline{AB} = 16$ feet.

2. ∠A ≅ ∠D as given in diagram.

    $\overline{AB} ≅ \overline{BD}$ as given.

    ∠ABE ≅ ∠DBC as equal vertical angles. (Vertical angles are formed by two intersecting lines. Opposite angles are equal and called vertical.)

    Therefore, Δ ABE ≅ Δ DBC by ASA. They are congruent. (The drawing is distorted.)

Practice, page 12.
1. Yes, they are congruent by the LL Property as two pairs of corresponding legs are given as equal.

2. Yes, they are congruent by the HL Property. One pair of corresponding legs is given as equal and they share the hypotenuse.

3. There is not enough information to be sure of congruency. There is an LA Property, but the A means equal corresponding angles other than the right angles.

Applications, page 15.
1. ∠ACB = ∠ECF as equal vertical angles.

    ∠ACB = ∠ECD as given.

    ∠ECD = ∠ECF since they are both congruent to ∠ACB (congruent angles).

    $\overline{CE} = \overline{CE}$ as it is the same line (congruent side).

    ∠CED = ∠CEF as they are both right angles (congruent angles).

    So Δ DEC ≅ Δ FEC by ASA or by LA as they are right triangles.

2. $\overline{HK} = \overline{IJ}$ as given equal sides of parallelogram.

    $\overline{KJ} = \overline{HI}$ as given equal sides of parallelogram.

    $\overline{HJ} = \overline{HJ}$ as it is the same line.

    So Δ HKJ ≅ Δ JIH by SSS.

3. No, the triangles are not necessarily congruent.

    $\overline{UT} ≅ \overline{WX}$ as given.

    ∠U ≅ ∠X as given.

    $\overline{TW} ≅ \overline{TW}$ as it is the same line.

This condition is SSA and doesn't guarantee congruency. We don't know for sure if $\triangle TUW \cong \triangle WXT$ without further measurements.

4. This is a situation where we can't be sure of congruency without further measurements.

$\overline{AE} \cong \overline{BD}$ as both measure 3.
$\overline{FE} \cong \overline{BC}$ as they both measure 3.5.
$\angle F \cong \angle C$ as they both measure 45.

But this conclusion is SSA, and we can't conclude that the triangles are congruent. The triangles could look like this:

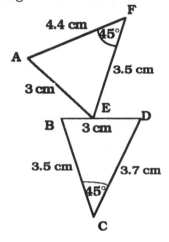

5.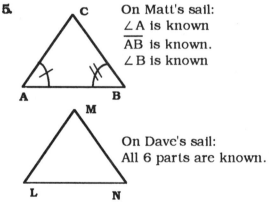

On Matt's sail:
$\angle A$ is known
$\overline{AB}$ is known.
$\angle B$ is known

On Dave's sail:
All 6 parts are known.

If $\angle A \cong \angle L$ and if $\angle B \cong \angle N$ and if $\overline{AB} \cong \overline{LN}$, then Matt's sail would be congruent to Dave's by ASA and Bob could give him the size of the other side.

6. Amy made two sides of the top triangle to be congruent to two sides of the bottom triangle. The angles formed by the intersecting lines are equal vertical angles. Therefore, the triangles are congruent by SAS and the hole measures 10 paces.

7. The pole is at a right angle to the ground. If the hypotenuse of each triangle is congruent, then the pole is at the center.

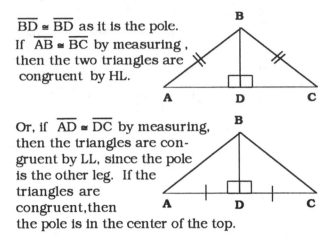

$\overline{BD} \cong \overline{BD}$ as it is the pole.
If $\overline{AB} \cong \overline{BC}$ by measuring, then the two triangles are congruent by HL.

Or, if $\overline{AD} \cong \overline{DC}$ by measuring, then the triangles are congruent by LL, since the pole is the other leg. If the triangles are congruent, then the pole is in the center of the top.

Chapter 2: Properties of Polygons

Practice, page 19.
Regular pentagon, regular hexagon, regular octagon, regular triangle (this is usually called an equilateral triangle), and a regular quadrilateral (this is called a square).

Practice, page 21 .
A. In figure A, two of the sides of the triangle do not add up to be greater than the third side. Thus, the triangle inequality says this figure can not be a triangle. $5 + 7 \not> 12$.

B. In figure B, the triangle inequality says the top of the figure can't be a real triangle since $3 + 3 \not> 8$.

C. In figure C, the midpoints of each side have been connected. The segments formed in the triangle are to be half the size of the side they are parallel to. But 5 isn't half of 12 and 5 isn't half of 14.

Proof, page 22.
Proof: If a trapezoid is isosceles, then the base angles are equal.

Draw auxilary lines to form right triangles. AD = BC as given **equal sides of isosceles trapezoid.**

DE = CF as lines drawn between parallel sides.

So, $\triangle AED \cong \triangle BFC$ by **HL as they are right triangles.**

We can conclude that ∠A = ∠B as corresponding parts of congruent triangles. Likewise, ∠ADC = ∠BCD.

Practice, page 23.

Since EF has been formed by connecting the midpoints of the sides, EF is equal to half the sum of the other two sides to which it is parallel.

$$EF = \frac{1}{2}(8 + 11)$$
$$EF = \frac{1}{2}(19)$$
$$EF = 9.5 \text{ cm}$$

Proof, page 25.

Proof: If HIJK is a parallelogram, then HE = EJ and KE = EI.

KJ = HI as given **equal opposite sides of a parallelogram**.

∠EHI = ∠EJK as alternate interior angles between parallel lines.

∠EIH = ∠EKJ as **alternate interior angles between parallel lines.**

So, △HEI ≅ △JEK by ASA.

We can conclude that HE = EJ as they are **corresponding parts of congruent triangles.**

Likewise, EI = EK as **corresponding parts of congruent triangles.**

Practice, page 26.

1. Given in the diagram that ∠A = 40°, then ∠C = 40° as the opposite angles of a parallelogram are equal. All the angles sum to 360°.

$$40° + 40° + D + B = 360°$$
$$80° + D + B = 360°$$
$$D + B = 280°$$

Since D and B are opposite angles with a sum of 280°, each angle measures 140°.

2. DE = EB as diagonals of a parallelogram bisect each other.
   ∠DEC = ∠BEA as vertical angles.
   CE = EA as diagonals of a parallelogram bisect each other.
   △DEC ≅ △AEB by SAS.

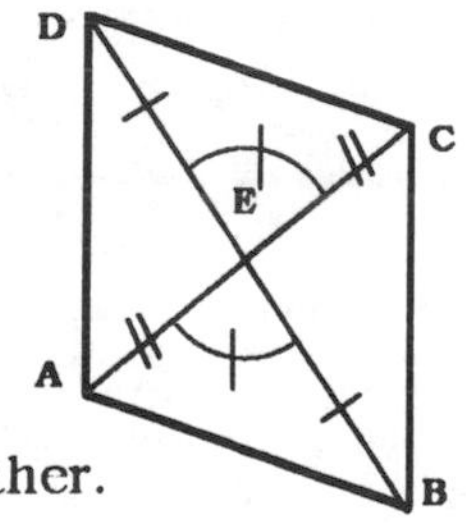

Proof, page 27.

Proof: If MNOP is a rectangle, then the diagonals are equal.

This proof will use the overlapping triangles PMN and ONM.

MN = MN as they are the same side of overlapping triangles.

PM = ON as **opposite sides of parallelogram are equal.**

∠PMN = ∠ONM given that the angles of a rectangle are right angles.

So, △PMN ≅ △OMN by **SAS** or by **LL** as they are right triangles.

We can conclude that PN = OM as corresponding parts of congruent triangles.

Practice, page 28.

1. Since BF is formed by connecting the midpoints of two sides of the triangle, it is parallel to CE. FD is also formed by connecting the midponts of two sides so it is parallel to AC.

   With BF∥CD and FD∥BC the figure is a parallelogram. Given it has a 90° angle, the parallelogram is a rectangle. Quadrilateral BFDC is a rectangle.

2. A rectangle has all the properties of a parallelogram; plus, it has angles that measure 90° and its diagonals are equal in length.

Practice, page 30.

No, it isn't a rhombus. Its diagonals are perpendicular to each other as in a rhombus. But the diagonals don't bisect each other, so we can't conclude that the figure is a parallelogram. A figure must be a parallelogram in order to be a rhombus.

Proof, page 31.

Proof: If QRST is a square, then all four sides are equal.

QE = SE as **equal bisected diagonals of a parallelogram**.

∠QER = ∠SET as **vertical angles**.

81

RE = TE as **equal bisected diagonals of a parallelogram**.

$\triangle$TES $\cong$ $\triangle$REQ by SAS and QR = TS as corresponding parts of congruent triangles.

Now show that adjacent triangles are congruent.

QE = ES as **equal bisected diagonals of a parallelogram**.

$\angle$QER = $\angle$SER as **they both equal 90° as perpendicular diagonals of a rhombus**.

ER = ER as **it is the same line**.

$\triangle$QER $\cong$ $\triangle$SER by **SAS** or by **LL as they are right triangles**. QR = SR as corresponding parts of congruent triangles.

Since QR = SR and QR = TS, then SR = TS and we can see that SR = TS = QR = TQ.

Practice, page 32.

Given that the diagonals are bisected, the figure is a parallelogram.

Given that the diagonals are perpendicular to each other, the parallelogram is a rhombus.

Given there is a right angle, the rhombus is a square with all sides equal to 6. The most specific name is a square.

Practice, page 34.

Sides	Angles	Triangles	Sum of Angles
4	4	2	2 x 180° = **360°**
5	5	3	2 x 180° = **540°**
6	6	4	4 x 180° = **720°**
7	7	5	5 x 180° = **900°**
8	8	6	6 x 180° = **1080°**
10	10	8	8 x 180° = **1440°**
N	N	N-2	(N-2)180°

Practice, page 35.

Sides	Sum all angles	Size each angle
4	(4-2) x 180° = **360°**	360°/4 = **90°**
5	**(5-2) x 180° = 540°**	540°/5 = **108°**
6	**(6-2) x 180° = 720°**	**720°/6 = 120°**
8	**(8-2) x 180° = 1080°**	**1080°/8 = 135°**
10	**(10-2) x 180° = 1440°**	**1440°/10 = 144°**
N	(N-2) x 180°	$\frac{\textbf{(N-2) x 180°}}{\textbf{N}}$

Practice, page 37.

1. First Method:

$$180° - 30° = 150°$$
$$\frac{(N-2) \times 180°}{N} = 150°$$
$$(N-2)\,180° = 150N$$
$$180N - 360° = 150N$$
$$30N = 360°$$
$$N = 360/30$$
$$N = 12 \text{ sides}$$

Second Method:
$$30N = 360°$$
$$N = 360/30$$
$$N = 12 \text{ sides}$$

2. **A.** Each exterior angle equals 90°. They sum to 360°.

 B. Each exterior angle equals 60°. They sum to 360°.

 C. Exterior angles are:
 X = 90°
 Y = 90°
 W = 130°
 Z = 50°
 They sum to 360°

 D. Exterior angles are:
 D = 40°
 E = 85°
 A = 80°
 B = 60°
 C = 95°
 They sum to 360°.

Applications, page 40.

1. $\frac{(20-2) \times 180°}{20} = 162°$

2. We could solve it two different ways. We can use the formula for the size of each angle and solve for the number of sides:

$$\frac{(N-2) \times 180°}{N} = 140°$$
$$(N - 2)x 180 = 140N$$
$$180N - 360 = 140N$$
$$180N - 140N = 360°$$
$$40N = 360°$$
$$N = 9 \text{ sides}$$

We could use the fact that all exterior angles must sum to 360°:

$$N \times 40° = 360°$$
$$N = 360/40$$
$$N = 9 \text{ sides}$$

3. The interior and exterior angles combine to form a straight angle, so they sum to 180°.

$$2X + X = 180°$$
$$3X = 180°$$
$$X = 180°/3$$
$$X = 60°$$

Now that we know the exterior angle is 60° and the interior angle is 120°, there are two ways to figure how many sides the polygon has:

$$\frac{(N-2) \times 180°}{N} = 120° \qquad N \times 60° = 360°$$
$$(N - 2) \times 180 = 120N \qquad N = 360/60$$
$$180N - 360 = 120N \qquad N = 6 \text{ sides}$$
$$180N - 120N = 360°$$
$$60N = 360°$$
$$N = 360/60$$
$$N = 6 \text{ sides}$$

4. With just a tape measure, Tom can't easily measure the corners to tell if they are 90°, but he could measure to tell if the opposite sides are equal. This would ensure that it is a parallelogram and not just a quadrilateral. And he could measure to see if the diagonals are equal. This would ensure that the parallelogram is a rectangle.

5. On the large triangle, the sides have been bisected and their midpoints have been connected. This line has half the measurement of the distance across the hole. The distance is 10 paces.

6. Based on triangle inequality, the third side would have to be 27.

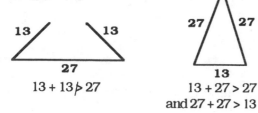

$$13 + 13 \not> 27 \qquad 13 + 27 > 27$$
$$\text{and } 27 + 27 > 13$$

7. Since EF is formed by connecting the midpoints of the sides , then EF is parallel to and equal to half of side AC, so EF = 3.

8. This drawing is distorted. The two non-parallel sides have the same measure. Thus, the trapezoid is isosceles and the base angles are equal. Angle X = 45°.

9. Figure A is a parallelogram because the diagonals bisect each other.

Figure B is not a parallelogram because only one diagonal has been bisected.

Figure C is a parallelogram because opposite sides are equal.

10. The figure is a parallelogram, given opposite sides are parallel.

The parallelogram can't have just one 90° angle. Opposite angles are equal so angle C is also 90°. Angles D and B are opposite and equal:

$$D + B + 90° + 90° = 360°$$
$$D + B + 180° = 360°$$
$$D + B = 360° - 180°$$
$$D + B = 180°$$

Since D = B, they both equal 90°.

Since the figure is a parallelogram and has 90° angles, the most specific name is a rectangle.

Chapter 3 Pythagorean Theorem

Practice, page 42.

1. $Y^2 = 12^2 + 5^2$
$Y^2 = 144 + 25$
$Y^2 = 169$
$Y = \sqrt{169}$
$Y = 13$

2. $8^2 + X^2 = 10^2$
$64 + X^2 = 100$
$X^2 = 100 - 64$
$X^2 = 36$
$X = \sqrt{36}$
$X = 6$

3. $T^2 + 3^2 = 5^2$
$T^2 + 9 = 25$
$T^2 = 25 - 9$
$T^2 = 16$
$T = \sqrt{16}$
$T = 4$

Practice, page 43.

1. Yes, it is a right triangle because:
$$16^2 + 30^2 = 34^2$$
$$256 + 900 = 1156$$
$$1156 = 1156$$

2. No, it is not a right triangle because:
$$2^2 + 3^2 \neq 3^2$$
$$4 + 9 \neq 9$$
$$13 \neq 9$$

Practice, page 45.

1. $d^2 = 9^2 + 5^2 + 4^2$
$$d^2 = 81 + 25 + 16$$
$$d^2 = 122$$
$$d = \sqrt{122}$$
$$d = 11.04$$

2. $d^2 = h^2 + w^2 + l^2$
$$d = \sqrt{h^2 + w^2 + l^2}$$

Practice, page 47.

1. $A = \frac{\sqrt{3}}{4} s^2$
$$A = \frac{\sqrt{3}}{4}(8^2)$$
$$A = \frac{\sqrt{3}}{4}(64)$$
$$A = \sqrt{3}(16)$$
$$A = 27.71$$

2. $A = \frac{\sqrt{3}}{4} s^2$
$$A = \frac{\sqrt{3}}{4}(10^2)$$
$$A = \frac{\sqrt{3}}{4}(100)$$
$$A = \sqrt{3}(25)$$
$$A = 43.30$$

Practice, page 48.

1. We can use the Pythagorean Theorem or the constant relationaship:

Pythagorean Theorem	Constant Relationship
$10^2 + 10^2 = h^2$	$h = \sqrt{2}\,L$
$100 + 100 = h^2$	$h = \sqrt{2}\,10$
$200 = h$	Hypotenuse $= 10\sqrt{2}$ cm
$\sqrt{200} = h$	
$\sqrt{2 \cdot 100} = h$	
$\sqrt{2} \cdot \sqrt{100} = h$	
$10\sqrt{2} = h$	

2.

Pythagorean Theorem	Constant Relationship
$L^2 + L^2 = 20^2$	Hypotenuse $= \sqrt{2} \times$ leg
$2L^2 = 400$	$20 = \sqrt{2}\,L$
$L^2 = 400/2$	$20/\sqrt{2} = L$
$L^2 = 200$	$14.14 = L$
$L = \sqrt{200}$	
$L = 14.14$	

Practice, page 50.

1. $S = \frac{1}{2} \times 2$ $L = \frac{\sqrt{3}}{2} \times 2$
   $S = 1$ $L = \sqrt{3}$

2. The hypotenuse is twice the short leg, H = 2 x 5. The long leg is $\frac{\sqrt{3}}{2}$ times the hypotenuse.
$$L = \frac{\sqrt{3}}{2} \times H$$
$$L = \frac{\sqrt{3}}{2} \times 10$$
$$L = 5\sqrt{3}$$

Applications, page 52.

1. The diagonal forms an isosceles right triangle. In a 45°-45°-90° triangle, the hypotenuse is equal to $\sqrt{2} \times$ leg, so:
$$6 = \sqrt{2} \times L$$
$$\frac{6}{\sqrt{2}} = L$$
$$4.24 = L$$

   This could have been solved by using the Pythagorean Theorem:
$$L^2 + L^2 = 6^2$$
$$2L^2 = 36$$
$$L^2 = 36/2$$
$$L^2 = 18$$
$$L = \sqrt{18}$$
$$L = 4.24$$

2. No, this can't be a right triangle. Check by using the converse of the Pythagorean Theorem:
$$4^2 + 4^2 \neq 6^2$$
$$16 + 16 \neq 36$$
$$32 \neq 36$$

3. Using the Pythagorean Theorem:
$$7^2 + 6^2 = h^2$$
$$49 + 36 = h^2$$
$$85 = h^2$$
$$\sqrt{85} = h$$
$$9.2 = h$$
It is 9.2 miles from start to end.

4. If the short leg is 8, then the hypotenuse is 16. The long leg is $\frac{\sqrt{3}}{2}$ times the hypotenuse, so it is $\frac{\sqrt{3}}{2} \times 16 = 8\sqrt{3}$.

5. No, the baton won't fit into the longest diagonal of the suitcase.

$$d = \sqrt{1^2 + w^2 + h^2}$$
$$d = \sqrt{20^2 + 14^2 + 8^2}$$
$$d = \sqrt{400 + 196 + 64}$$
$$d = \sqrt{660}$$

d = 25.68. The longest diagonal is only 25.69 and the baton is 26 inches.

6. We can use the Pythagorean Theorem to solve for the hypotenuse of a right triangle with home plate forming the right angle:

$$90^2 + 90^2 = B^2$$
$$8100 + 8100 = B^2$$
$$16,200 = B^2$$
$$\sqrt{16,200} = B$$

127.27 = B The ball traveled 127.27 feet.

7. Using the constant relationship in a 30°-60°-90° triangle, the guy wire is the hypotenuse and the roof measurement is the long leg.

long leg is $\frac{\sqrt{3}}{2}$ times the hypotenuse

$$7 = \frac{\sqrt{3}}{2} H$$
$$7 = .866 H$$
$$7/.866 = H$$
$$8.08 = H$$

The guy wire should be 8.08 feet long.

8. On the 30°-60°-90° triangle, the hypotenuse is 15. The height above the ramp is the short leg.

short leg = $\frac{1}{2}$ x hypotenuse

height = $\frac{1}{2}$ x 15

height = 7.5 feet

9. A diagonal from one corner to the opposite corner forms an isosceles right triangle. The diagonal can be found using the Pythagorean Theorem or the constant relationship on a 45°-45°-90° triangle:

Pythagorean Theorem

$$30^2 + 30^2 = d^2$$
$$900 + 900 = d^2$$
$$1800 = d^2$$
$$\sqrt{1800} = d$$
$$42.43 = d$$

Constant Relationship

$$d = \sqrt{2} \times \text{leg}$$
$$d = \sqrt{2} \times 30$$
$$d = 30\sqrt{2}$$
$$d = 42.43 \text{ yards}$$

10. Use the formula for the area of an equilateral triangle. Let S = 10.

$$A = \frac{\sqrt{3}}{4} S^2$$
$$A = \frac{\sqrt{3}}{4} 10^2$$
$$A = \frac{\sqrt{3}}{4} 100$$
$$A = \sqrt{3} \; 25$$
$$A = 43.30 \text{ ft}^2$$

Chapter 4 Measurement

Practice, page 55.

1. P = 2 + 5 + 2 + 4 + 4 = 17

2. $P = 2\frac{1}{2} + 2\frac{1}{2} + 6\frac{1}{2} + 6\frac{1}{2} = 18$

3. C = 2πR
C = 2 π4
C = 8π
C = 25.12

4. This is a rectangle and a half circle with a diameter of 4 inches and a radius of 2 inches. The perimeter is the sum of half the circumference and the four sides of the rectangle.

$$P = \frac{1}{2}(2\pi 2) + 8 + 6 + 6 + 4$$
$$P = 2\pi + 24 = 6.28 + 24 = 30.28 \text{ inches}$$

5. A rhombus has four equal sides.
P = 4 x 3.25
P = 13 feet

Practice, page 59.

1. Since the side measuring 9 inches is perpendicular to the side measuring 12 inches, the area is : A = $\frac{1}{2}$ x 9 x 12 = 54 square in.

To find the perimeter use the Pythagorean Theorem to find the size of the hypotenuse.
$$9^2 + 12^2 = 225$$
The hypotenuse is 15 inches. Thus,
P = 12 + 9 + 15 = 36 inches.

2. The diameter is 22 centimeters so the radius is 11 centimeters.

C = 2πr
C = 2π 11
C = 22π
C = 69.08 cm

A = πr²
A = π 11²
A = π121
A = 379.94 cm²

3. $A = \frac{1}{2} \times H \times (a + b)$ $P =$ sum of all sides

$A = \frac{1}{2} \times 8 \times (7 + 11.2)$ $P = 7 + 9.5 + 11.2 + 8$

$A = \frac{1}{2} \times 8 \times 18.2$ $P = 35.7$ cm

$A = 72.8$ sq. cm

4. A photograph is rectangular.

$A = L \times W$ $P = 2L + 2W$

$A = 3 \times 5$ $P = 2 \times 5 + 2 \times 3$

$A = 15$ sq. in $P = 16$ in

5. Divide the shape into a parallelogram with a square on the top and bottom ends.

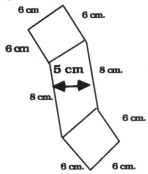

The area is the sum of the parallelogram and two squares.

$A = B \times H$ plus $A = S^2$ plus $A = S^2$

$A = 8 \times 5$ + $A = 6^2$ + $A = 6^2$

$A = 40$ +   36   +   36

$A = 112$ sq. cm

The perimeter is the sum of three sides of each square and two sides of the parallelogram.

$P = 6 \times 6$ plus 2×8

$P = 36$ +   16

$P = 52$ cm.

Practice, page 62.

1. $V = \frac{1}{3} \times 9 \times 24 = 72$ cubic in.

2. $V = 4 \times 3 \times 6 = 72$ cubic cm.

3. The radius is 5 yards. $V = \frac{4}{3} \times \pi 5^3 = 523.3$ yd^3

4. $V = \frac{1}{3} \times 5 \times \pi 1.5^2 = 11.775$ cubic inches

5. $V = 3 \times \pi \, 1.25^2 = 14.71875$ cubic inches

Applications, page 64.

1. $P = 2(8\frac{1}{2}) + 2(11) = 39$ inches

$A = 8\frac{1}{2} \times 11 = 93.5$ in^2

2. Since $P = 4S$

$28 = 4S$

$28/4 = S$

$7 = S$ Each side is 7 m. The area is:

$A = 7^2 = 49$ square meters.

3. $A = 15 \times 15 = 225$ square feet.

$225 \times \$5.95 = \$1338.75$.

4. This is a rhombus with two right triangles. All the sides of the rhombus measure 4.3 cm. The hypotenuse of each right triangle is also 4.3 cm. The triangles have a leg of 2.5 cm. Use the Pythagorean Theorem to find the other leg:

$4.3^2 = 2.5^2 + L^2$

$3.498 = L$

The perimeter is the sum of both legs of the two triangles and two sides of the rhombus.

$P = 2(4.3) + 2(3.498) + 2(2.5) = 20.596$ cm.

5. $V = 8 \times 3 \times 3 = 72$ cubic feet

6. Given the circumference we can find the radius.

$C = 2\pi r$

$14 = 2\pi r$

$7 = r\pi$

$\frac{7}{\pi} = r$

$2.23 = r$

The volume is:

$V = H \times \pi \, r^2$

$V = 6 \times \pi \times 2.23^2$

$V = 93.68$ cubic inches

7. The tube is a cylinder 12 inches long and a radius of 2 inches. The two ends make one sphere that has a radius of 2 inches.

Volume = cylinder + sphere

$V = 12 \times \pi 2^2$ + $\frac{4}{3} \pi r^3$

$V = 48\pi$ + 10.7π

$V = 184.31$ cubic inches

8. The radius is half of 8.5 meters or 4.25 meters. The top area is:

$A = \pi \times 4.25^2$

$A = 56.71625$ m^2

The distance around is the circumference:

$C = 2\pi r$

$C = 2\pi \times 4.25$

$C = 26.69$ m

9. Volume of a pyramid is: $V = \frac{1}{3} \times H \times$ area of base. The area of the base is the area of an equilateral triangle which can be found using the formula:

$A = \frac{\sqrt{3}}{4} S^2$

$V = \frac{1}{3} \times 4.5 \times (\frac{\sqrt{3}}{4} 2^2)$

$V = \frac{1}{3} \times 4.5 \times 1.732$

$V = 2.598$ cubic inches

10. The area of the base is:

$A = \frac{1}{2} \times 3.75 \times (4.5 + 6)$

$A = 19.6875$ square centimeters

The volume of the prism is:

$V = 18 \times 19.6875$

$V = 354.375$ cubic centimetrers

Chapter 5 Similarities of Polygons

Practice, page 66.

The ratios of the corresponding sides are:

$\frac{9}{6} = \frac{12}{8}$

These ratios simplify to 3/2.

Practice, page 67.

The triangles are similar by AAA. The scaling factor can be found by setting up the ratios of the corresponding sides.

$\frac{3}{1} = \frac{3\sqrt{3}}{\sqrt{3}} = \frac{6}{2}$

All of these ratios simplify to 3/1.

Practice, page 68.

The triangles are not similar because the sides are not all proportional.

$\frac{4}{2} = \frac{4}{2} \ne \frac{6}{2.5}$

We can't be sure that angle Y = 58° without further information.

Practice, page 69.

The triangles are similar by SAS. $\angle Z = 30°$, since $180° - 75° - 75° = 30°$. The corresponding sides forming the 30° angles are proportional:

$\frac{22}{18} = \frac{22}{18}$

The side $\overline{XY}$ will also be proportional to side $\overline{AB}$. The scaling factor of the triangle on the right to the triangle on the left is $\frac{22}{18}$, which simplifies to $\frac{11}{9}$.

Find side $\overline{XY}$ by setting up a ratio of $\frac{XY}{AD}$ equal to the scaling factor:

$\frac{N}{12} = \frac{11}{9}$

$9N = 12 \times 11$

$N = 14.6$ Side $\overline{XY} = 14.6$.

Applications, page 70.

1.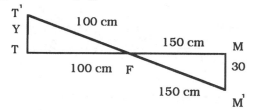

$\triangle T^1FT \sim \triangle M^1FM$ by SAS, so the sides are proportional.

$\frac{150}{100} = \frac{30}{Y}$ Y = 20 cm

2. Yes, $\triangle UTV \sim \triangle STR$ by SAS because $\overline{UT} = 8$, $\overline{TV} = 8$, $\overline{RT} = \overline{ST} = 14$, and the sides are proportional.

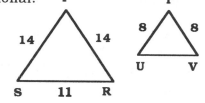

The included angles between these proportional sides are the same. The scaling factor of the small triangle to the large triangle is $\frac{8}{14}$ or $\frac{4}{7}$. Side $\overline{UV}$ and $\overline{SR}$ will be proportional: $\frac{4}{7} = \frac{Y}{11}$.

$7Y = 4 \times 11$

$7Y = 44$

$Y = \frac{44}{7}$ or 6.28   Side $\overline{UV} = 6.28$.

3. The three triangles are $\triangle ABC$, $\triangle ADB$, and $\triangle BDC$. All three are similar to each other by AAA.

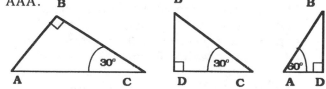

4. Given two equal angles, the third angles are also equal. The triangles are similar by AAA. Y can be found by setting up ratios of corresponding sides.

$\frac{10}{5} = \frac{Y}{8}$

$Y = 16$

X can be found using the Pythagorean Theorem.

$$10^2 + 16^2 = X^2$$
$$100 + 256 = X^2$$
$$356 = X^2$$
$$\sqrt{356} = X$$
$$18.86 = X$$

Practice, page 71.

The scaling factor is the ratio of corresponding sides: $\frac{33}{22} = \frac{27}{18} = \frac{13.5}{9}$. These ratios simplify to 3/2 or 1.5.

The perimeter of $\triangle ABC$ is 49 feet. The perimeter of $\triangle DEF$ is 73.5 feet. The ratio of 73.5/49 simplifies to 3/2 or 1.5.

Practice, page 72.

The scaling factor is 3/2 because $\frac{4.5}{3} = \frac{6}{4} = \frac{7.5}{5} = \frac{3}{2}$. The ratio of perimeters equals $\frac{3}{2}$ because $\frac{18}{12} = \frac{3}{2}$. The ratio of the area equals $(\frac{3}{2})^2$ or $\frac{9}{4}$ or 2.25 because $\frac{13.5}{6} = \frac{9}{4}$ or 2.25.

Practice page 73.

The three dimensions are the same on a cube. The ratio of volumes is $\frac{64}{8}$ which simplifies to $\frac{8}{1}$. This is the cube of the scaling factor.

$$\left(\frac{2}{1}\right)^3 = \frac{8}{1}.$$

Applications, page 74.

1. The scaling factor for the polygon on the right to the polygon on the left is 20/7. The ratio of corresponding sides will equal 20/7:

$$\frac{20}{7} = \frac{Y}{10.5}$$
$$210 = 7Y$$
$$30 = Y$$

2. The perimeter of the large polygon is 120 m. The perimeter of the smaller is 42 m. The ratio of perimeters is 120/42. This simplifies to 20/7 which is the scaling factor.

3. The scaling factor of the large trapezoid to the small trapezoid is 2/1. The ratio of the areas is equal to $(\frac{2}{1})^2$ or 4.

$$\frac{\text{area of large}}{\text{area of small}} \qquad \frac{Y}{5} = \frac{4}{1}$$
$$Y = 20$$

The area of the large trapezoid is 20 sq. m.

4. The scaling factor is 3/1. The ratio of volumes will be $(\frac{3}{1})^3$ or 27.

$$\frac{\text{volume of large}}{\text{volume of small}} \qquad \frac{27}{1} = \frac{Y}{75.36}$$
$$Y = 27 \times 75.36$$
$$Y = 2034.72 \text{ cu. in}$$

5. $\frac{22}{3} = \frac{Y}{1.36}$
$3Y = 22 \times 1.36$
$3Y = 29.92$
$Y = 9.97$ mm

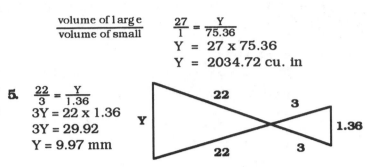

6. $\frac{6}{1} = \frac{4}{Y}$
$6Y = 4$
$Y = \frac{4}{6} = \frac{2}{3}$ The box is lifted $\frac{2}{3}$ of a foot.

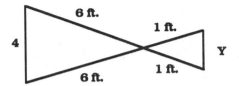

7. The scale factor for the large shape to the small shape is $2\frac{1}{3}$ to 1. The height of the door is a linear dimension and the ratio of corresponding linear dimensions will equal the scaling factor.

$$\frac{\text{large}}{\text{small}} \qquad \frac{2\frac{1}{3}}{1} = \frac{7}{Y}$$
$$2\frac{1}{3} Y = 7$$
$$Y = 3$$

The height of the door on the dog house will be 3 feet.

8. The scale factor is 3. The ratio of areas will be $(\frac{3}{1})^2$ or 9.

$$\frac{9}{1} = \frac{Y}{80}$$
$$Y = 9 \times 80$$
$$Y = 720 \text{ square inches}$$

9. Adding a brace will form similar triangles.

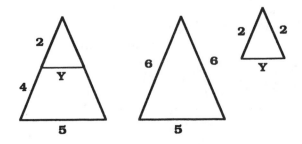

Set up a ratio of corresponding sides to solve for the missing side.

$$\frac{6}{2} = \frac{5}{Y}$$
$$10 = 6Y$$
$$\frac{10}{6} = Y$$

The brace should be $1\frac{2}{3}$ feet long.

10. The scaling factor is $2/1$. The amount of cookies it contains is the volume that would increase by the cube of the scaling factor. $(\frac{2}{1})^3$ is 8.

$$\frac{\text{large}}{\text{small}} \qquad \frac{8}{1} = \frac{Y}{30}$$
$$Y = 8 \times 30$$
$$Y = 240$$

The large box would hold 240 cookies.

Final Assessment Test, page 77.

1. **A.** The figure is an isosceles right triangle or a 45°-45°-90° triangle.
   B. The figure is a rhombus because all four sides are equal and the diagonals are perpendicular.
   C. The figure is a parallelogram because the diagonals are bisected.
   D. The figure is a rectangle because the diagonals are bisected and congruent.

2. Volume = $5 \times 5 \times 7 = 175\ cm^3$
   The longest diagonal is:
   $$d^2 = 5^2 + 5^2 + 7^2$$
   $$d^2 = 25 + 25 + 49$$
   $$d^2 = 99$$
   $$d = \sqrt{99}$$
   $$d = 9.949\ cm$$

3. **A.** This is a quadrilateral, so all interior angles sum to 360°.
   $$90° + 2x + 30° + 2x = 360°$$
   $$4x + 120° = 360°$$
   $$4x = 240°$$
   $$x = 60°$$

   B. The angles sum to 180°.
   $$90° + 52° + x = 180°$$
   $$142° + x = 180°$$
   $$x = 38°$$

   C. x is the exterior angle that forms a straight angle with the missing third angle.
   $$180° - 20° - 25° = 135°$$
   $$x + 135° = 180°$$
   $$x = 45°$$

4. To find the area of a right triangle, use the legs that are perpendicular to each other. Use the Pythagorean Theorem to find the other leg.
   $$9^2 + y^2 = 11^2$$
   $$81 + y^2 = 121$$
   $$y^2 = 40$$
   $$y = \sqrt{40}$$
   $$y = 6.32\ m$$

   To find the area, use the base of 9 m and the height of 6.32 m.
   $$A = \frac{1}{2} \times 9 \times 6.32$$
   $$A = 28.46 \text{ square meters}$$

5. **A.** True
   B. False. A rectangle doesn't have four equal sides.
   C. False. The diagonals of a rhombus are perpendicular but not always equal in length.
   D. False. Only on a 30°-60°-90° triangle is the short leg half the length of the hypotenuse.

6. The height of $\triangle ABD$ is $\overline{ED}$ which equals:
   $$6^2 + h^2 = 10^2$$
   $$36 + h^2 = 100$$
   $$h^2 = 64$$
   $$h = 8$$

   Notice that $\triangle BFD \cong \triangle BED$ by ASA, since: $\angle EBD = \angle FBD$, given $\overline{BD}$ is a shared side, and $\angle BDE = \angle BDF$ as equal third angles. So $\overline{DF} = 8$ and $\overline{BF} = 6$ as corresponding parts of congruent triangles.

   Area of $\triangle ABD = \frac{1}{2} \times 8 \times (9) = 36$
   Area of $\triangle BDC = \frac{1}{2} \times 8 \times (10) = 40$
   Area of $\triangle ABC = 36 + 40 = 76$ square inches

7. Opposite angles are equal in a rhombus, so $\angle D = \angle B = \angle 135°$ and $\angle A = \angle C = 45°$ (360° - 135° - 135° = 90° + 2 = 45°).

   The right triangle $\triangle DEC$ is a 45°-45°-90° triangle, so the hypotenuse is $\sqrt{2}$ times a leg.

   $$6 = \sqrt{2} \times H$$
   $$\frac{6}{\sqrt{2}} = H$$
   $$4.24 = H$$

   The height of the rhombus is 4.24 and the base is 6. Since the rhombus is a parallelogram, the area = base x height.

   $A = 6 \times 4.24 = 25.44$ square feet.

8. The area equals $\frac{1}{2}$ x 4 x (6 + 10) = 32 sq. m.

The perimeter is the sum of sides. Find the two unmarked sides by using the Pythagorean Theorem.

$2^2 + 4^2 = y^2$
$4 + 16 = y^2$
$20 = y^2$
$\sqrt{20} = y$
$4.47 = y$

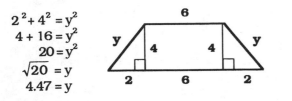

The perimeter is 4.47 + 6 + 4.47 + 10 = 24.94 m.

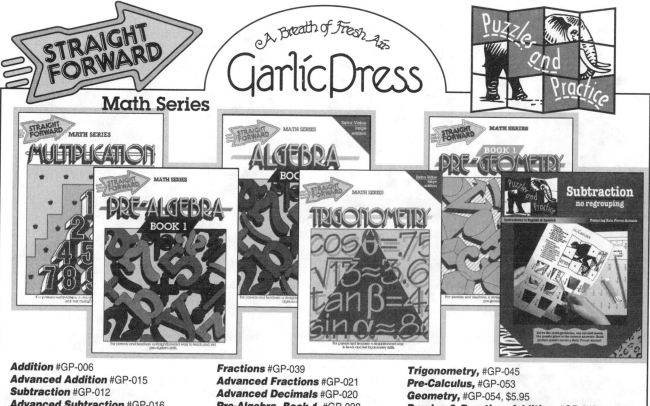

English Series

The **Straight Forward English Series** is designed to measure, teach, review, and master specific English skills: capitalization and punctuation; nouns and pronouns; verbs; adjectives and adverbs; prepositions, conjunctions and interjections; sentences; clauses and phrases; and mechanics.

Each workbook is a simple, straightforward approach to learning English skills. Skills are keyed to major school textbook adoptions.

Pages are reproducible.

GP-032 **Capitalization and Punctuation**
GP-033 **Nouns and Pronouns**
GP-034 **Verbs**
GP-035 **Adjectives and Adverbs**
GP-041 **Sentences**
GP-O43 **Prepositions, Conjunctions, & Interjections**

ADVANCED SERIES, large editions
GP-055 **Clauses & Phrases**
GP-056 **Mechanics**

Substitute Teaching

GP-027 Substitute Teacher Folder

A pertinent information folder left by regular classroom teachers listing class schedules, classroom procedures, discipline, support personnel, and regular classroom teacher expectations.

GP-001 Substitute Ingredients

A collection of imaginative language arts, math, and art activities for grades 3–8. Reproducible master sheets accompany most lessons.

GP-002 Mastering the Art of Substitute Teaching

Substitute teaching formats, strategies, and activities strictly from practical experience.

GP-003 Classroom Management for Substitute Teachers

Suggested procedures for being-in-charge, establishing rapport, and getting the support of regular classroom teachers and staff.

GP-014 Lesson Plans for Substitute Teachers

A packet of 12 lesson plan forms to be filled out by regular classroom teachers to provide one day of instruction during their absence.

GP-004 Just Fun

Engaging, high-interest activities that are short span, 10-15 minutes in length.